CW01337740

Happy birthday dear

have fun

Brian

❧ TRADITIONAL ❧ COUNTRY CRAFTS

TRADITIONAL COUNTRY CRAFTS

SUE MILLARD

PHOTOGRAPHY BY DEREK WILLIAMS

ILLUSTRATIONS BY JANE FENEMORE

STRUIK

Struik Publishers (Pty) Ltd
(a member of The Struik Publishing Group (Pty) Ltd)
Cornelis Struik House
80 McKenzie Street
Cape Town
8001

Reg. no. 63/00203/07

First published in 1993

Copyright © text, illustrations and photographs Sue Millard 1993

Editing Elizabeth Frost
Design Janice Evans and Petal Palmer
Cover design Janice Evans
Photography Derek Williams
Photographic styling Marine Williams
Illustrations Jane Fenemore
Line drawings Clarence Clarke
Layout Darren McLean

DTP conversion by BellSet, Cape Town
Reproduction by Unifoto (Pty) Ltd, Cape Town
Printed and bound by South China Printing Co., Hong Kong

ISBN 1 86825 341 4

All rights reserved. No part of this publication may be reproduced, stored in a retrieval
system, or transmitted, in any form or by any means, electronic, mechanical,
photocopying, recording, or otherwise, without the prior written permission of the
copyright owner.

ACKNOWLEDGEMENTS

Once again, I am indebted to so many people for their help and support, and would like to extend my grateful
thanks to them all: my husband Phil, for his patience, encouragement and support; my children Alexandra and
Nicholas for cooking so many meals; Alexandra for candlewicking the mirror surround; Nicholas for making the
corner cupboard; my daughter Belinda for making the beautiful patchwork balls and Father Christmases; Phil,
my son Garrick, Jenny, Anne Finnegan and Jacques Honner for transporting me to various venues; Daphne
Dean of Biggie Best, Gundi Köhler of Dainty Daisy, Andrea van Niekerk of Martha's Vineyard, Stephry and
Tinika Geldenhuis of Antiek-Antiek, Linda Godlonton of Knitting Nook, Lance and Margaret Goodale of
Victorian Bathrooms, Clarewood Antiques, Eléanor Watson of the Wynberg Wool Shop, Jeanette Hawkins,
Paddy Lee, Marlene Lancaster, Joan Huisamen, Susha Young, Maureen van Dam, Joy Hollman, Mrs van Laar,
Melody Moore, Barbara Court, Dalene Louw, Shirley Wittridge and Anne le Maitre for the loan of many props
and for helping in various ways; Frances le Maitre, Kimberley Williams, and Phoebe and Lily Lawson for
modelling the children's garments; Barry and Irene Coldicott, Anne and Chris Finnegan, Sheba and Ted du
Plooy, Professor and Mrs Dickie, Peter and Nini Bairnsfather-Cloete, Ampie and Petal Muller, the manager and
staff of De Ouwe Werf guesthouse in Stellenbosch, and Victorian Bathrooms of Claremont, for very kindly
providing locations for photography; Janice Evans and Petal Palmer for all the time and effort spent designing
the book and arranging photography; Elizabeth Frost for her amazing patience, encouragement and very
precise editing; Jane Fenemore for the beautiful illustrations; Clarence Clarke for drawing the patterns; Marine
Williams for her creative styling; Derek Williams for his patience and really beautiful photographs; the Presby
Youth and the Monday evening Bible Study group for their encouragement and prayerful support, and, once
again, all the cats and the dog for staying awake with me when I had to work through the night.

• CONTENTS •

THE BASICS ◆ 7

PART 1: **TECHNIQUES**

Embroidery ◆ 13

Candlewick Embroidery ◆ 19

Smocking ◆ 23

Quilting ◆ 31

Working with Lace ◆ 37

PART 2: **SEWING PROJECTS**

General Techniques ◆ 42

For the Bedroom ◆ 45

For the Bathroom ◆ 73

For the Living-room ◆ 77

For the Nursery ◆ 85

Clothing for Babies and Children ◆ 93

Decorations and Gifts ◆ 101

PART 3: **PATTERNS AND TEMPLATES** ◆ 113-159

INDEX ◆ 160

◆ THE BASICS ◆

The main reason for writing this book was to encourage you to take your beautiful heirloom linen, that requires careful laundering, out of the linen cupboard and to use it to make projects that require very little care and attention. Large bedspreads or tablecloths, for example, can be made into beautiful curtains; embroidered or crocheted doilies can be made into simple Christmas decorations; lacy traycloths can be made into lovely cushion covers. These are just a few ideas. After paging through the book, you will, I hope, feel inspired to make all manner of beautiful articles for your family and home.

If you have not inherited old sheets, fabric or antique lace, don't be put off making the projects; modern fabric and lace, which are easily obtainable from haberdashery shops, can be substituted very successfully.

The book is divided into three sections, namely, general and specific needlework techniques, easy-to-make projects and, lastly, all the designs and patterns required to complete the projects.

MATERIALS AND EQUIPMENT

FABRIC

As a general rule, buy the best quality fabric that is available. Good quality fabric has a close, even weave; is completely colourfast; does not shrink; and is easily washed. Linen, 100 per cent cotton, silk, and cotton and polyester blends are all suitable fabrics for the projects described in this book. All fabric should be washed and ironed before using (*see* below).

NOTE *When making the projects, readers are advised to use either the metric or the Imperial measurements given, and not a combination of the two.*

PREPARING THE FABRIC
Unshrunk calico or cotton fabric
Place the entire piece of fabric in a bath of plain, cold water overnight. Hot water will 'cook' the starch into the fabric so that you will not be able to remove it; as a result, the fabric will be too stiff. It is important not to add any washing powder or fabric softener to the water—the fabric lying below the surface of the water will be bleached by the washing powder, whereas the fabric lying above the water-line will not be bleached because of the air pockets that form.
   The next day, wash the fabric in the washing machine on the hot cycle, using a mild washing powder and fabric softener. Press while still damp.

Pre-shrunk calico or cotton fabric
Wash the fabric in the washing machine on a hot washing cycle, using washing powder and fabric softener. Press while still damp.

WADDING

Wadding, also known as batting, is used in English quilting and for quilting candlewicked projects, to create a raised effect. It is available in various thicknesses, for example, 68–100 g (2¼–3½ oz), which is light-to medium-weight wadding. Be sure to use sheet wadding and not polyester stuffing, which is used for stuffing cushions and similar items. For most quilted projects a light-weight wadding is the most suitable and easiest to use.

It is sometimes necessary to join two or more pieces of wadding in order to achieve the desired width and length. One way of doing this is by overlapping the edges of the two pieces, halving the thickness of each so as not to create extra bulk, and slip-stitching the edges together (*see* Fig. 1).

side view

two layers overlapping each other

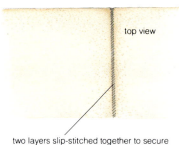
top view

two layers slip-stitched together to secure

Fig. 1

NEEDLES

A large variety of needles is available and as specific types of needles are required for the different needlework techniques, they have been described in greater detail in the appropriate chapters.

It is important to store all needles in a dry place to prevent rusting.

A useful tip to remember when threading a needle, is to cut the thread only once the needle has been threaded, to prevent unravelling.

PINS

Good pins are important. Use sharp, fine, rustproof, stainless steel pins and discard any that are bent, rusty or blunt. Glass-headed pins are useful as they are easy to see.

FOR LEFT-HANDED PEOPLE
Left-handers should follow the instructions given for right-handers, simply substituting 'left' for 'right' and 'right' for 'left', and reversing the direction in which the stitches are worked in the diagrams.

SCISSORS

It is a good idea to have several different types of scissors for different purposes. Embroidery scissors are essential for fine, accurate work and cutting off threads. A sharp pair of dressmakers' scissors is useful for cutting fabric. It is also a good idea to keep an old pair of scissors especially for cutting out templates and paper.

THIMBLE

Using a thimble will prevent your fingers from becoming painful, particularly when you are using fine needles and thick fabric.

Different types of thimbles are available for various techniques, but an ordinary metal thimble is quite suitable for most purposes.

EMBROIDERY AND QUILTING HOOPS

Working on a hoop gives a more even, professional finish to any quilted, embroidered or candlewicked project as it is much easier to make neat, even stitches, and to prevent puckering, if the fabric is held taut.

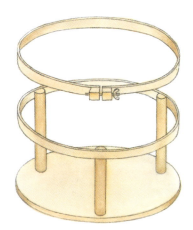

Fig. 2

Using the hoop

To use the embroidery hoop, remove the outer ring, and place the fabric over the inner ring, making sure that you centre the design within the hoop. Replace the outer ring, tighten the screw and pull the fabric taut. Do not keep the fabric tightly stretched in the hoop over long periods of time as this may distort the fabric; it is better to loosen the outer ring or remove the fabric between work sessions.

HINT If the fabric for the project to be worked is too small to fit across the hoop, enlarge it by sewing a piece of interlining or scrap fabric to each of the four sides. Remove the extra fabric once the project is complete.

THE NARROW HEMMING FOOT

The narrow hemming foot, which is available for most sewing machines, is used to make a neat, narrow hem on a single layer of fabric.

THE RUFFLER FOOT

If you are going to make lots of ruffled items—for instance, the frills on cushions, curtains, and so on—it is a good idea to buy a ruffler foot, which should be obtainable for most sewing machines. It will gather metres and metres of ruffles in a few moments.

Using the narrow hemming foot

1. Sew a few straight stitches, close to the edge of the fabric, then reverse and sew another few stitches in the opposite direction. Remove the fabric from the machine, and cut the threads, leaving lengths of 5 cm (2 in). (It is important to have these threads to hold on to, so that you can guide the fabric easily through the coil of the foot; *see* Fig. 3.) This will become easier with practice, and will save a great deal of time.

2. The needle on most sewing machines can be moved to the right or to the left. Move the needle slightly to the right, so that it will not slip off the edge of the hem. Holding the loose threads, pull the edge of the fabric through the coil of the foot and release the presser foot. Allow the cut edge of the fabric to rest in the 'ditch' on the upper side of the foot.

3. Now sew the hem, gently easing the fabric through the foot with your left hand, while at the same time guiding it and preventing it from slipping off the foot with your right index finger.

NOTE It is not advisable to use the narrow hemming foot when working with lace as the threads of the lace will become caught in the coil of the foot.

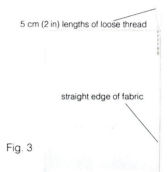

5 cm (2 in) lengths of loose thread

straight edge of fabric

Fig. 3

Using the ruffler foot

It is essential that you have the uses of this foot demonstrated to you when you buy it. Here are three additional hints that will make using the ruffler foot easier:

◆ Use only the very best sewing thread available. It will not break easily and will prevent the foot from 'jamming'. Find out from the manufacturer which brand best suits your machine.

◆ After you have attached the foot to the shank of the machine, and before you tighten the screw, place the index and middle fingers of your left hand underneath the bottom end of the shank and the piece of the foot that hooks around the shank, and lift them as high as possible. Then tighten the screw on the shank. There will now be a space between the bottom blade of the foot and the teeth of the machine. This allows the blade to move freely, which makes it work more efficiently.

◆ It is essential to leave a short length of thread to hold on to.

It is important to set aside an area for sewing. In this pretty, old-fashioned sewing room we see candlewick and quilting projects in progress.

THREAD

The threads most suitable for each of the techniques are described in the appropriate chapters.

Whichever technique you are using, I suggest that you make a sampler and experiment with different threads, to ascertain which type and thickness of thread best suits you, before you begin work on any project. Cut an old piece of calico or any plain fabric about 40 cm (16 in) square, place it securely in the hoop, and pull it taut (*see* page 9). Now practise the stitches you intend using in single threads of different types, and then try using double threads. It is advisable to work with fairly short threads that are no longer than the distance from the tip of the fingers to the elbow, as long threads are inclined to knot and wear thin, or even break. You can also try using two or three strands of silky embroidery cotton combined with a matt knitting cotton, or perhaps two or three different shades of embroidery cotton together.

NOTE *Before using coloured thread, make sure that it is colourfast by washing it in very hot water.*

Check the tension of your work to ensure that the stitches and knots are lying flat and secure on the fabric; they should not be floppy or loose.

TRACING MEDIUM

Use a water-soluble marking pen for tracing designs on to fabric. This is the only kind of pen worth using as the ink remains on the fabric only until the square is washed. Marks made by other felt-tip or ballpoint pens can be impossible to remove.

When tracing a design on to felt use dressmakers' carbon of a contrasting colour. Place the felt on a flat surface, put the carbon (right side down) on the felt and then place the embroidery design on top of the carbon. Draw over the design; the design will be traced on to the felt.

INSPIRATION FOR DESIGNS

Creating your own designs for embroidery, candlewicking or quilting is very easy and will give you a great sense of achievement, particularly when you see the completed project. Designs do not have to be complex to be successful; very often, the simpler they are, the better.

If you do not feel confident in your ability to draw freehand, perhaps you might like to do the same as I do: I pick flowers and leaves of different shapes and sizes and iron them flat and dry between two pieces of brown paper. I then use these flattened shapes as templates.

To create a design, move the shapes around on a piece of paper until you have a pretty arrangement, then draw around the shapes. Do not throw these 'templates' away when you have finished; instead, lay them flat in a covered container and store them until you feel inspired to create another design.

Beautiful porcelain plates and fabrics are another source of inspiration to me. In the photograph on page 18 you will see a rose, a cup and saucer, an embroidery design and an embroidered picture mount in a hoop. This design was inspired by the beautiful crockery and the roses, wisteria and forget-me-nots that were growing in my garden. (No, I did not catch a butterfly and iron it flat, I just used my imagination!)

If you are a little hesitant about co-ordinating colours, find a plate, a piece of fabric or a picture that gives you pleasure each time you look at it. Take it to your local haberdashery shop and ask an assistant to help you choose the colours and threads that will create the right effect. Once you have gained confidence you will be able to experiment with colour and texture and create designs using your own colour combinations.

TRACING THE DESIGN ON TO THE FABRIC

Before tracing the design, it is very important to find the centre of the fabric and of the design, so that you can position the design accurately on the fabric.

To find the centre of the piece of fabric you are working on, fold it in half vertically and then in half horizontally. Draw your thumbnail across the folds to make a crease. Now measure the design at its widest point, from the extreme left to the extreme right and find the halfway mark. Draw a vertical line at the halfway mark. Turn the design round and do the same from top to bottom. The point at which the lines cross is the centre point of your design.

Place the centre point of the fabric over the centre point of the design and carefully pin the paper and fabric together so that the centre points do not shift. If the design is dark enough you will be able to see it right through the fabric. If it is not dark enough, use a felt-tip pen to darken it before pinning the two layers together. Trace the design on to the fabric in a solid line using a water-soluble pen.

Another way of tracing a design on to fabric is to stick the design and the fabric—once you have found and marked their centre points—to a window-pane with sticky tape and then trace the design.

A third method is to use a glass-topped coffee table or to rest a piece of glass on two blocks (one block beneath either side of the glass) and place a torch or bedside light underneath the glass. Place the centre point of the fabric over the centre point of the design, on top of the glass, stick them both down with tape, and trace the design on to the fabric. The design shows up very clearly with the light shining beneath it and is therefore easy to trace.

If you intend doing a great deal of work that will involve tracing designs in this way, invest in a piece of Perspex, which is unbreakable.

NOTE *You may come across designs for candlewicking projects in which the dots are unevenly spaced. This inaccuracy will be clearly visible once the embroidery is complete. If the dots on the design you are using are unevenly spaced, use dressmakers' carbon and a tracing wheel to trace the outline of the design on to the fabric. This will produce a series of accurately spaced dots. Work the knots (French, bullion or colonial) on every second mark made by the tracing wheel. However, this does depend on the thickness of the thread; with very fine thread you would work a knot on each mark.*

ENLARGING OR REDUCING A DESIGN

The easiest way to enlarge or reduce a design is on a photocopy machine, but for those who don't have access to one, it is best to use the grid method. Draw an evenly squared grid over the design. Then draw another, separate, grid, with the same number of squares as the first, making the squares larger or smaller, depending on the size you would like the design to be. Now copy the design on to the larger or smaller grid, square by square (*see* Fig. 4b).

Fig. 4a

Fig. 4b

The right tools are the key to successful sewing.

TOP ROW, FROM LEFT TO RIGHT: *stranded embroidery thread, twisted embroidery thread, cotton perlé, metallic thread, candlewicking thread, thick wool used for Italian quilting, quilting thread, quilting thimble, scissors, tape measure.*

MIDDLE ROW, FROM LEFT TO RIGHT: *pins, metal thimble, quilting, chenille and crewel needles, needle threader, ruffler foot, zipper foot, narrow hemming foot, cotton insertion lace, satin ribbon, zips.*

BOTTOM ROW, FROM LEFT TO RIGHT: *graph paper, tracing paper, wadding, water-soluble pen, embroidery hoop on stand, fabric—from top to bottom—huckaback, linen, calico, silk, lawn.*

· EMBROIDERY ·

Since biblical times people have been decorating fabric and creating beautiful articles for their homes and for wearing.
For many centuries it was considered important for women to be competent in embroidery, and girls were taught the skills from an early age. Although this practice has died out since Victorian times, embroidery still enjoys considerable popularity today, across a wide spectrum of ages and cultures.
Simple embroidery, using only a few basic stitches, is very effective when decorating items of any size, from small projects such as handkerchiefs, to complete room settings. Embroidery is very therapeutic as it allows one to be creative, and is a craft that absolutely everyone, both young and old, can enjoy because it is so easy.
In this book, we have covered only three of the vast number of embroidery techniques, namely, basic embroidery, candlewick embroidery and smocking. In this chapter we focus on the techniques and stitches of basic embroidery.

MATERIALS AND EQUIPMENT

FABRIC

See The Basics on page 8 for information on the selection and preparation of fabric for embroidery.

WASHING AND IRONING EMBROIDERED FABRIC

Wash the embroidered fabric in warm water using a mild, pure soap powder. Try not to rub the embroidery as this may cause the stitches to overlap one another, particularly in the case of satin or fishbone stitch. Rinse the fabric thoroughly and roll it gently in a towel to remove the excess water.

Embroidered fabric should be ironed while still damp. Place a towel, folded double, on the ironing board. Place the embroidered project face down on the towel so that the embroidery is supported, and iron the project from the back, using a moderately hot iron. Be careful not to scorch the fabric.

NEEDLES

Needles of many different types and sizes are available and you will need to keep a variety on hand for the different kinds of embroidery you do. The higher the number of the needle, the finer it is. Crewel needles have a fine, sharp point and a narrow eye and should be used for fine embroidery.

SCISSORS

Embroidery scissors should be small and have sharp, finely tapered points.

THIMBLE

See The Basics, page 8.

EMBROIDERY HOOP

See The Basics, page 8.

THREAD

Six-strand embroidery cotton is probably the most popular of all the available embroidery threads. It comes in a wide range of colours and is extremely versatile, as one can separate the strands and use them singly for a very delicate effect

(*see* the feather stitch on the butterfly's wing in the photograph on page 18), or two or more strands may be used to create a bolder effect.

Cotton perlé is another very popular thread, which is available in 15 m (16 yd) skeins and 10 g (0.35 oz) balls in a variety of thicknesses. It is soft and silky and a pleasure to use as it pulls through the fabric easily.

Metallic threads are also available and may be used to highlight parts of a design, such as the fine veins on a butterfly's wings, rays of sunlight falling softly on a flower or even the delicate patterns in a peacock's feathers.

Fine crochet cotton may also be used successfully.

TRACING MEDIUM

See The Basics, page 10.

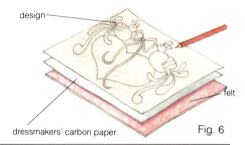

Fig. 6

design

felt

dressmakers' carbon paper

BEGINNING AND ENDING OFF THE EMBROIDERY

It is always preferable not to have knots at the back of fine embroidery. Instead, begin by leaving a short length of embroidery thread on the right side of the fabric and, working on the inside of the design, work two or three small running stitches towards the starting point of the design; then begin the embroidery (*see* Fig. 5a).

Fig. 5b

To finish off, run the needle under several stitches at the back of the work (*see* Fig. 5c).

When the embroidery is complete, carefully pull the loose ends of the threads through to the back of the fabric and work them away into the existing stitches.

NOTE *Do not 'jump' from one part of the design to another using the same piece of thread as it will probably be visible on the right side of the fabric. It is better to finish off each motif before moving on to the next.*

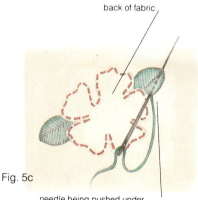

back of fabric

Fig. 5c

needle being pushed under several stitches to finish off motif

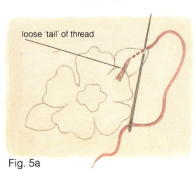

front of fabric

loose 'tail' of thread

Fig. 5a

Fig. 5d

EMBROIDERY STITCHES

In this chapter we cover the most commonly used embroidery stitches, attempting to provide a selection that will enable you to achieve a variety of effects when completing the projects in this book or projects of your own.

Those stitches traditionally associated with candlewicking—the French knot, the colonial knot (an elaborate French knot), satin stitch, back stitch, chain stitch and stem stitch—have been covered in the chapter on candlewick embroidery, on pages 20–21.

Blanket stitch is an open buttonhole stitch, which is worked from left to right. It is worked in exactly the same way as the buttonhole stitch (*see* below), except that a space is left between each stitch. The spacing between the stitches may vary, depending upon the effect you wish to create. I often use this stitch to outline the wings of a bird.

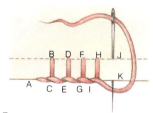

Fig. 7

Bullion stitch is best worked on fabric that is stretched in a hoop, leaving both hands free to work the stitch.

Bring the needle to the front at B and insert it a short distance away at A. Allow the needle to re-emerge at B but do not pull it through completely. Wrap the thread around the needle six or seven times, place the left thumb on the coil formed, and pull the needle through carefully. Insert the needle at A to secure the stitch.

To finish off, work two or three back stitches (*see* page 20) on the reverse side of the fabric.

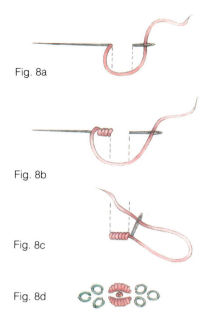

Fig. 8a

Fig. 8b

Fig. 8c

Fig. 8d

Buttonhole stitch is a lovely stitch that can be worked in circles or scallops, or in a straight line. It is often used as an edging stitch in 'white work'.

Keep the needle vertical and work along the line from left to right. Come out just below the line at A, insert the needle at B and come out at C. Pull the needle through, keeping the thread below the point of the needle. Hold the thread down with the middle finger of the left hand and insert the needle at D, coming out at E. Continue in this manner until the area to be covered is complete.

Finish off by taking the thread over the last stitch and pulling the thread through to the back of the work; then run the needle under several stitches.

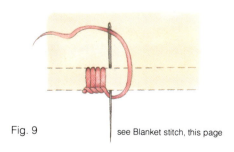

Fig. 9   see Blanket stitch, this page

Cable stitch can be used to embroider any shape that requires a 'brickwall' effect. It is worked from left to right *along* the line of the design, not above and below the line.

Bring the thread through to the front, on the line (A), and insert the needle a little to the right, again on the line (B). Bring the needle out to the left, midway along the length of the stitch, with the thread below the needle (C). The next stitch is worked in the same way, but with the thread above the needle.

To finish off, run the needle under a few stitches at the back of the work.

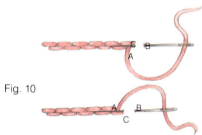

Fig. 10

Coral stitch is a knotted stitch worked from right to left that I use to embroider butterflies' feelers and the stamens of flowers.

Bring the thread through the fabric at A, lay the thread along the line of the design, and hold it down with your left thumb. Go in at B and come out at C, with the thread looped below the line, as shown. Pull the thread through to form a small knot. Secure the last knot by pulling the needle through to the back of the work, next to the knot.

To finish off, run the needle under a few stitches at the back of the work.

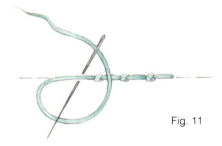

Fig. 11

Feather stitch is a quick, decorative stitch that makes an attractive feathery line, whether worked on straight lines or along curves. I often use it to embroider hearts, and the veins of leaves and butterflies.

Working from top to bottom along the centre line, bring the thread up at A. Hold the thread down with the left thumb. Go in at B and come out at C, making a small slanted stitch towards the centre line, and keeping the thread below the point of the needle. Pull the needle and thread through. Go in at D, hold the new loop down and make a small slanted stitch towards the centre line, keeping the thread below the point of the needle and coming out at E. Pull the needle and thread through. Continue in this manner, alternating from left to right. Secure the last stitch by bringing the thread over the loop and pulling the needle through to the back of the work. To finish off, run the needle under several stitches at the back of the work.

Fig. 12

Fishbone stitch can be used to embroider leaves and the bodies of butterflies and is worked from top to bottom along the centre line of the design.

Bring the thread through at A. Insert the needle at B. Pull the needle and thread through at C. Reinsert the needle just below B and pull the needle and thread through at D. Continue working from the centre to the right and then from the centre to the left until the design is complete. Work the stitches evenly and closely together so that no fabric shows through.

To finish off, run the needle under a few stitches at the back of the work.

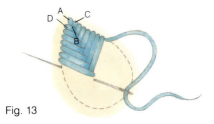

Fig. 13

Lazy daisy stitch (or **Detached chain stitch**), if worked in a circle, makes a lovely flower, and if worked singly, makes very pretty leaves. If a bolder effect is required, work one detached chain stitch inside another.

To make a daisy, come out at A, form a loop with the thread, and reinsert the needle at A, coming out at B inside the loop. Pull the thread through, keeping the looped thread below the point of the needle. Reinsert the needle at C and come out at D (at the centre of the circle).

Form a loop with the thread and reinsert the needle at D, coming out at E inside the loop. Pull the thread through, keeping the looped thread below the point of the needle. Reinsert the needle at F and come out at the centre of the circle again at G. Continue in this manner until a circle of lazy daisy stitches has been worked. Come up right in the middle of the circle and make a French knot (*see* page 21).

To finish off, run the needle under a few stitches at the back of the work.

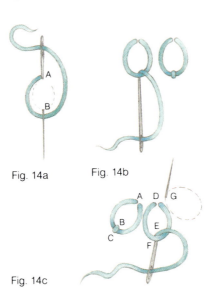

Fig. 14a   Fig. 14b

Fig. 14c

Long and short stitch is useful for shading large or irregular shapes and, if done correctly, no fabric should show through.

Bring the needle through from the back at A and reinsert it at B, bring it out again at C and reinsert it at D.

Continue in this way, forming a row of alternating long and short stitches and closely following the outline of the shape. The second and following rows are worked in long stitches only. Come up at the *top* of the spaces between the long stitches worked in the previous row.

Finish off by running the needle under several stitches at the back.

Fig. 15

Outline stitch is worked from left to right, in the same way as stem stitch (*see* page 21) except that the thread is held above the line of the design.

Come out at A. Hold the thread above the line of the design, go down at B, and come up at C. Go down at D and come up at E. Continue in this manner, keeping the stitches equal in length. On a curve, make your stitches smaller to accommodate the curve.

Finish off by running the needle under several stitches at the back.

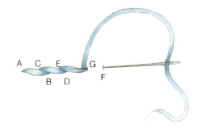

Fig. 16

Pekinese stitch is created using a back stitch, which is interlaced with stitches that form a looped edge.

Work a row of back stitches (*see* page 20) from right to left. Then, working from left to right, bring the needle through from the back just below A. Push the needle upwards under BC and, leaving a loop, push the needle downwards under AB. Pull the thread gently to tighten the loop. Now, push the needle upwards under CD and, again leaving a loop, push the needle downwards under BC. Repeat until sufficient stitches have been worked.

Finish off by running the needle under several stitches at the back.

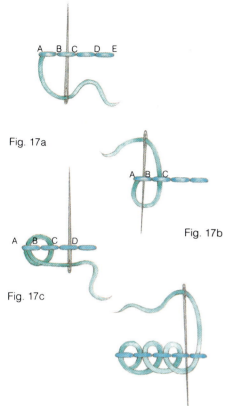

Fig. 17a

Fig. 17b

Fig. 17c

Fig. 17d

Roumanian stitch is a long, closely worked filling stitch worked from the top to the bottom of the design.

Come out at A, go in at B, and out again at C, about halfway across the design and just above AB. Make a small diagonal stitch over AB and go in at D, coming out at E, and forming CD, which is a securing stitch. Go in at F and come out at G, just below the first slanted stitch, and make a small slanted stitch over EF, going in at H and coming out at I. Continue in this manner, keeping the slanted stitches even down the centre of the design.

Secure the last straight stitch by bringing the thread over the stitch. Pull the needle through to the back and run it under several stitches.

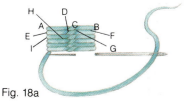

Fig. 18a

Fig. 18b

Running stitch is a small, straight stitch that is worked from right to left, with even spaces between stitches.

Fig. 19

Scroll stitch, which is worked from left to right, forms a wave-like line that makes an attractive border.

Bring the thread through at A. Loop the thread in a circle as shown and hold the circle of thread down firmly with the left thumb. Make a small slanted stitch inside the circle of thread, going in at B (just above the line) and coming out at C (just below the line). Pull the thread through gently and tighten. Continue until the desired number of stitches has been worked. Finish off by bringing the thread up and over the circle of thread and pulling the needle through to the back of the work. Run the needle under several stitches.

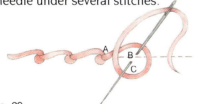

Fig. 20

Sheaf stitch is an attractive filling stitch. Begin by working three or four vertical stitches (AB, CD, EF) side by side. Push the stitches to the right, and hold. Bring the needle to the front at G. Release the stitches. Feed the needle under the stitches from the right, bringing it out to the left of AB. Wrap the thread around the vertical stitches twice, taking care not to pierce the fabric, and end by reinserting the needle at G.

To finish off, work a couple of back stitches (see page 20).

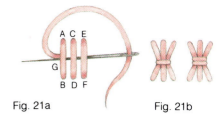

Fig. 21a   Fig. 21b

Threaded running stitch is a very attractive and versatile stitch.

First, work a row of running stitches (see above) from right to left. Then, beginning on the right, weave a second length of thread in and out under each of the running stitches as shown, leaving the thread fairly loose.

Finish off by running the needle under several stitches at the back.

Fig. 22

Twisted chain stitch is worked from right to left. Bring the thread to the front at A. Move the thread above the line and hold it down with the forefinger of your left hand. Form a loop with the thread and reinsert the needle at B, making a small slanted stitch towards the line, and coming up at C inside the loop. Pull the thread through, keeping the looped thread below the point of the needle. Move the thread above the line, hold it down with the forefinger of your left hand, and reinsert the needle at D, making a small slanted stitch towards the line and coming up at E inside the loop. Pull the thread through, keeping the looped thread below the point of the needle. Continue until the row of stitches is complete.

Secure the last loop by bringing the thread over the loop and pulling the needle through to the back. Run the needle under several stitches.

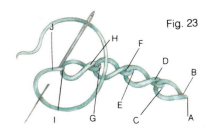

Fig. 23

.CANDLEWICK. EMBROIDERY

Candlewicking is a very simple but beautiful form of embroidery that is said to have originated in America. In fact, it had far earlier beginnings in Europe, as it was the immigrants from the various European countries that took with them to America their basic knowledge of embroidery. Out of circumstance and thrift a rather coarse, but very beautiful, type of embroidery was born.

It appears that the designs of the early needlewomen were inspired by their surroundings, as indeed are the candlewicked designs in this book.

Candlewicking is easy to do and, as a fairly thick thread is used, one can see progress very quickly. Needless to say, this is encouraging to novices and experienced enthusiasts alike.

MATERIALS AND EQUIPMENT

FABRIC

Candlewick embroidery was originally done on unshrunk 100 per cent cotton calico. Once the embroidery was complete the calico was washed in very hot water, and this would cause the fabric to shrink and thus hold the embroidery stitches firmly in place. Each damp square was then stretched on a blocking frame until it was quite dry before being made into the chosen article. The fabric was never ironed, giving the candlewicked project that traditional puckered look.

Today we have lovely fabrics on the market, including very good quality 100 per cent cotton calico that is available both pre-shrunk and unshrunk. Although the unshrunk fabric is usually rather stiff, it does wash very well.

Wash and iron the fabric as described in The Basics on page 8 before beginning work on your project. It is particularly important to do so at this stage if you plan to quilt your candlewicked project as quilted work should never be ironed.

NOTE *Many people use a polyester and cotton blend curtain lining for candlewicking. The warp thread of this kind of fabric is made from cotton, and the weft thread, from polyester. Because the cotton is inclined to shrink, this fabric should be prepared in the same way as unshrunk calico (see page 8).*

WADDING

Wadding, which is also known as batting, is used for quilting candlewicked projects. See The Basics on page 8 for information on the most suitable thickness and weight to select and on how to go about joining two or more pieces of wadding, should you require a piece that is longer or wider than what you have, or can purchase, for the project that you are making.

NEEDLES

You will need a sharp, large-eyed, sturdy needle such as a No. 22 Chenille needle or a No. 7 crewel embroidery needle for candlewicking. A tapestry needle is unsuitable as it tends to snag the fabric.

SCISSORS

See The Basics, page 8.

THIMBLE

See The Basics, page 8.

THE HOOP

It is essential to use a hoop for candlewick embroidery. Buy a 30 cm (12 in) or 35 cm (14 in) quilting hoop as this can be used for embroidery as well as for quilting. Having the hoop mounted on a base will leave both hands free to do the embroidery.

THREAD

Although specially manufactured candlewicking thread is not always obtainable, there are many suitable substitutes. For example, various types of 100 per cent mercerized cotton and embroidery cotton are most suitable and any of the embroidery stitches worked in these threads look beautiful. I prefer to use a matt, four-ply 100 per cent knitting cotton for working the knots, but try using a combination of shiny and matt cottons to produce an interesting texture.

I often use two or three different types of thread to candlewick the designs on a quilt, using the thicker matt knitting cotton double to accentuate important sections.

For the more delicate embroidery stitches, it is best to use No. 5, No. 8 or any cotton thread of a similar thickness. Although it is not traditional, I have, on occasion, also used a No. 5 acrylic crochet thread. It washes extremely well and looks very pretty. On the other hand, you might like to candlewick your quilt traditionally, using only one type of matt thread throughout.

Check the tension of your work to ensure that the knots are lying flat and secure on the fabric. They should not be floppy or loose as this will make the work look untidy.

TRACING MEDIUM

See The Basics, page 10.

CANDLEWICKING STITCHES

Antique candlewicked quilts seen in American museums reveal that the stitches used most frequently by early American candlewickers were large French knots, satin stitch and back stitch. Several other stitches were added later, for example, colonial knots (larger than the French knot), chain stitch and stem stitch.

The division between embroidery and candlewicking stitches is not as hard and fast as it used to be and many different stitches can be incorporated most successfully into your candlewicking designs. (*See* Embroidery Stitches on pages 15–17 for a wider range of stitches.)

Back stitch is worked from right to left. Bring the needle up at A. Go down at B and come back up at C. Go down at A and come up at D. Continue in this manner, making all the stitches equal in length.

To finish off, run the needle under a few stitches at the back of the work.

Fig. 24

Chain stitch is ideal to use on heavy outlines. Working from right to left, bring the needle up through the fabric at A. Form a loop with the thread and reinsert the needle at A, coming up at

B inside the loop. Pull the thread through, keeping the looped thread below the point of the needle. Make a loop and reinsert the needle at B. Come up at C, which is inside the loop, and pull the thread through as before, keeping the looped thread below the point of the needle.

To finish off, secure the last loop by bringing the thread over the loop and pulling the needle through to the back of the work. Run the needle under several stitches.

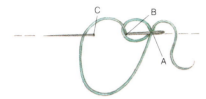

Fig. 25

Colonial knots are worked from left to right. Bring the thread to the front of the fabric at A. Holding the thread and needle as you would for a French knot (see below) push the needle under the thread from left to right, then take the thread over and under the point of the needle to form a figure of eight. Reinsert the needle to the right of where it first emerged, pulling the needle and thread through to the back of the fabric and tightening the knot in exactly the same way as you would do the French knot (see below).

Finish off by running the needle under several stitches at the back of the work.

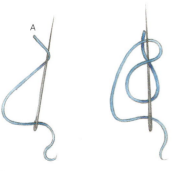

Fig. 26a   Fig. 26b

French knots are worked from left to right. Bring the needle through from the back to the front of the fabric. Hold the thread towards you, between the left thumb and forefinger. Hold the needle between the right thumb and forefinger. Wrap the thread around the needle once and insert it just to the right of where the thread first emerged, pull the needle and thread through to the back of the work, and let the loop formed rest over your left thumb or forefinger. Move your thumb or finger about to adjust the shape and tension of the knot. Slip the loop off your finger at the last moment and continue to pull the needle and thread through to the back until the knot rests firmly on the fabric, then come up through the fabric again to execute the next knot.

To finish off, run the needle under a few stitches at the back of the work.

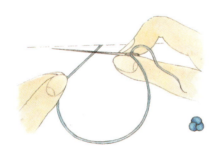

Fig. 27

NOTE *The thread may be used double to produce larger knots.*

When the thread is wrapped around the needle twice, the stitch is called a bullion knot, which should not be confused with the bullion stitch (see page 15).

Satin stitches are straight stitches that are worked closely together, evenly and neatly. Begin across the centre of the design and work towards the end of the design. Turn the work around, feed the needle under the stitches at the back, until you reach the middle, and then complete the other half. Try not to overlap any of the stitches.

To finish off, run the needle through the stitches at the back of the work.

Fig. 28

Stem stitch is worked from left to right. Come up at A. Hold the thread below the line of the design, go down at B and come up at C. Go down at D and come up at E. Continue in this manner, keeping the stitches equal in length. Make your stitches smaller to accommodate any sharp curves.

Finish off by running the needle under several stitches at the back.

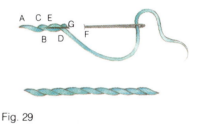

Fig. 29

QUILTING CANDLEWICKED PROJECTS

Quilting adds texture and depth to any project, and warmth to articles like tea cosies, bed covers and jackets. Should you wish to quilt your candlewicked project, work a back stitch (see page 20) under each knot using cotton of the same colour as the fabric. It is not advisable to use a running stitch next to your candlewicking stitches as this can look very untidy.

· SMOCKING ·

Smocking is an embroidery technique that is used to control the fullness of a garment by means of gathers or pleats that are held in place by rows of decorative stitching.

The smock was originally worn by women as an undergarment but was later adapted to be worn as an outer, protective garment. As smocks were very practical, they were worn by farmers and labourers alike. Children were also used as labourers and they, too, wore smocks.

The front and back panel, and the top of the sleeves, of these garments were gathered and stitched, and the garments were often also heavily and beautifully embroidered. Many can still be seen in museums today.

Towards the end of the last century, fewer men wore smocks but it became fashionable for women and children to wear smocked garments. Today, the word 'smocking' conjures up images of little girls wearing pretty dresses, but there are many other interesting and creative ways to use this technique, a few of which are demonstrated in the projects section.

MATERIALS AND EQUIPMENT

FABRIC

Select a good quality fabric with an even weave for smocking. Loosely woven fabric looks untidy and the pleats do not always pull up evenly. Cotton, cotton mixtures, fine woollen mixtures, linen, silk and cotton velvet are amongst those fabrics that are suitable.

All fabric used for smocking should be completely washable and not too springy—fabric with a high nylon content, for example, is not a good choice—as the pleats will pop out to form bubbles.

Small-patterned prints, as well as plain fabrics, or even a combination of both, look quite charming when smocked, particularly when they are made up into garments for children.

Bear in mind that, generally, smocking will reduce a piece of fabric to about one third of its original width, depending on the tension of your embroidery.

When buying fine fabric such as lawn, remember that you will need extra fabric across the width of the garment because fine fabric will pull up tighter and more pleats will be required to cover the area.

Wash and iron the fabric as described in The Basics on page 8 before you begin smocking.

To gather the fabric into pleats in preparation for smocking you will need smocking dot transfers or a smocking pleater (*see* below).

NEEDLES

Choose a needle that is best suited to the type of fabric and thread to be used. The needle should have a sharp point and a large eye (a No. 7 or No. 8 crewel needle is an excellent choice); a blunt needle will snag the fabric.

SCISSORS

See The Basics, page 8.

THIMBLE

See The Basics, page 8.

THREAD

The choice of embroidery thread depends on the weight of the fabric and the effect you wish to obtain. There are basically two types of embroidery threads: stranded thread and unstranded or twisted thread.

Stranded thread—such as *coton à broder*—consists of six separate strands that may be used in various thicknesses, depending on the weight of the fabric and how bold you wish the design to be. For most fine to medium-weight fabrics use three or four strands; for heavier fabrics as many as six strands may be used.

To ensure that the strands lie next to one another neatly, hold on to one end of the thread, making sure that the ends are even, and run your thumbnail and forefinger along the length of the thread several times.

Unstranded or twisted thread—such as cotton perlé—is made in various thicknesses, the most popular being No. 5 and No. 8. Once again, the thickness you use will depend on the weight of the fabric and the boldness of the design.

The approximate length of thread you will need for one row is about three times the width of the row. If the thread is too long it will begin to fray and look untidy.

THE SMOCKING PLEATER

If you are expecting to do a great deal of smocking, it is well worth buying a smocking pleater. It is a wonderful little machine that simultaneously draws up many rows of gathering threads and saves a considerable amount of time. Smocking pleaters are made in various sizes; the number of needles determines the size of the pleater.

IMPORTANT *Read the manufacturer's instructions, supplied with the pleater, before using your pleater for the first time.*

SMOCKING DOT TRANSFERS

Smocking dot transfers are printed in various sizes. Select the spacing that best suits the weight of the fabric you have chosen. The wider spacing is suitable for medium- to heavy-weight fabrics, while the narrow spacing is more suitable for fine fabrics. The wider the spacing between the dots, the more fabric you will require.

A smocking pleater—note that the needles are pointing towards you—with prepared fabric being fed through the machine on to the gathering threads.

Using the smocking pleater

1. Before preparing to pull up the pleats, ensure that the top edge of the fabric is quite straight by pulling a weft thread out and cutting along the line that is formed. Then press the fabric.

2. Put the smocking pleater on a table with the needles pointing towards you. Adjust the spacing of the needles on your pleater to half or full spacing, depending on the weight of the fabric you are using. (Fine fabric, such as that used for making infant garments, should have smaller pleats than heavier fabric.) Always allow one extra row of pleats at the top and bottom of the panel to be smocked (for example, if 12 rows are to be embroidered, thread 14 needles), as it is much easier to work the embroidery stitches if the fabric above the first row and below the last row is held firmly in place. Remove the needles that will not be used; this will prevent snags and holes, which will be difficult to remove.

3. Use strong thread of a contrasting colour to the fabric and cut it into lengths of about 50 cm (20 in). Thread the required number of needles, double the thread, and make a large knot at the end of each double thread. If the thread is dark, you will find it much easier to thread the needles if you place a piece of white paper on top of the base of the pleater.

4. Put the fabric on the table, and align the left-hand end of the dowel with the left edge of the fabric. Fold the fabric very slightly over the dowel and tape it firmly to the dowel along its length. Now, making absolutely certain that the grain of the fabric (running from left to right) is quite straight, carefully roll the fabric onto the dowel. Rest the dowel with the rolled up fabric on the bottom of the loops at the back of the pleater. Carefully ease the front edge of the fabric between the two back rollers, hold the dowel with your left hand, and turn the handle on the right side of the pleater slowly. If you turn the handle too fast the needles might break. Gently hold the dowel and feed the fabric through the rollers and on to the needles, as evenly as possible. At all

times, make sure that the grain of the fabric is straight. As the needles fill up with pleats, gently ease them on to the threads.

5. When all the fabric has been pleated, push the fabric to the knotted ends of the threads and cut the other ends of the threads off, close to the needles. Adjust the pleats so that they are uniform and lie close together without becoming crushed. They should not be pulled up too loosely because it will be difficult to embroider the pleats evenly and neatly.

6. Tie each pair of gathering threads securely together, and check that they are all the same length (i.e. that the panel to be smocked is the same width from top to bottom). Trim the excess threads to 4–5 cm (1½–2 in). The pleated panel should by slightly narrower than the measurement of the completed article because once the panel has been smocked and the gathering threads withdrawn, the panel will stretch slightly. Adjust the pleats so that they lie absolutely straight from top to bottom. Do not remove the gathering threads until the smocking is complete.

Using the dot transfers

1. Decide how deep the smocked panel will be, work out how many rows of gathering threads there will be, and carefully plan the smocking design accordingly. Then cut the smocking transfer sheet to size, allowing an extra row of dots at the top and bottom of the transfer sheet. To ensure that the top edge of the fabric is quite straight, pull a weft (crosswise) thread out and cut along the line that is formed. Stay-stitch the fabric if it frays easily. Test that the transfer dots do not show on the right side of the fabric, which they might do on fine fabric. In this case it would be better to use a smocking pleater.

2. Cut away the manufacturer's name from the transfer sheet. Place the right side of the transfer sheet on top of the wrong side of the fabric, ensuring that the top edge of the transfer sheet and the fabric are aligned. Pin, tape or tack the transfer sheet to the fabric.

3. Transfer the dots on to the fabric by firmly ironing the transfer once with a warm iron (do not use steam). Make sure that you iron right into the corners. Carefully remove the transfer paper.

4. Using strong thread of a contrasting colour, cut lengths about the width of the fabric, plus 15–20 cm (6–8 in). You will need one thread for each row of dots. Thread the needle, double the thread and make a large knot at the end.

5. Working from right to left and beginning on the wrong side of the fabric, pick up each dot by inserting the needle on one side of the dot and pushing it out on the other side of the same dot. Each row of dots is picked up in exactly the same manner. Leave the excess double gathering thread hanging loose at the end of each row.

6. When all the rows of dots have been picked up, pull all the pairs of gathering threads gently until the pleats lie closely and uniformly together without becoming crushed. Check that the pleated panel is the same width from top to bottom. Tie each pair of gathering threads together so that the pleats will not pull out. Trim the threads to 4–5 cm (1 ½–2 in). (The pleated panel should be slightly narrower than the measurement of the completed article, as once the panel has been smocked and the gathering threads withdrawn, the panel will stretch slightly.)

Fig. 30

7. Adjust the pleats so that they lie absolutely straight from top to bottom. Steam the pleats to set them by holding a steam iron above the fabric—but not touching the fabric—before you begin smocking. The gathering threads will be removed once the smocking is complete.

This smocked cushion illustrates a variety of attractive smocking stitches (see pages 26–29).

PLANNING AND POSITIONING THE DESIGN

Before you begin the embroidery, you will need to plan the pattern carefully and draw the plan on graph paper. Make sure that your design is balanced from top to bottom, and from left to right.

It is important that the larger, central motif be correctly centred on the pleated panel. To do this, count the number of pleats and mark the centre pleat. Count the number of gathering threads and mark the centre thread. The gathering threads will be used as guidelines along which you will work the embroidery stitches. Centre the middle of the central motif on the centre pleat, then work towards the edges of the fabric. The smaller designs above and below this central motif should be planned and positioned in the same manner.

NOTE *It is always a good idea to use a row of stitches that will secure the pleats as the first and last rows of a pattern. Stem stitch, outline stitch and single and double rows of cable stitch, which are described later in this section, are all suitable.*

SMOCKING STITCHES

To begin smocking, thread the needle and knot the end of the thread. Start at the back of the work and bring the needle up through the third pleat. (Leave two pleats unsmocked at the beginning and end of each row to allow for a seam to be sewn when you complete the project.) Using whichever stitch you have chosen (*see the selection on this and the next few pages*), work from left to right (for most stitches), keeping the needle parallel to the gathering thread. Pick up each pleat with your needle (in the way described for the particular stitch you are using), about halfway between the top of the pleat and the gathering thread and pull the thread gently until it rests snugly on top of the pleat. Pick up the pleats one at a time and keep the tension even throughout. Work the embroidery stitches just above or below the gathering threads as it is difficult to withdraw the gathering threads if they are caught in the embroidery thread.

If you run out of thread before the end of a row, push the needle through a dip between two pleats to the back of the work. Work two or three back stitches (*see page 20*) on top of a pleat at the back, close to where your needle emerged. Rethread your needle, make a knot at the end, and bring the needle through to the front of the work in exactly the same place as you pushed it to the back. Continue smocking.

Finish off the row by taking the needle to the wrong side of the work and securely working two or three back stitches on the top of the third pleat from the end. Trim the thread.

NOTE *If you make a mistake, unpick the embroidery stitch with the eye of the needle as soon as you notice it. Do not be tempted to leave the mistake as it will be noticeable once the article is complete.*

Bullion stitch roses, which are pretty and decorative, are worked across two or more pleats (in Fig. 31 we have used four pleats) as follows: bring the needle up on the left-hand side of the first pleat. Insert the needle on the right-hand side of the fourth pleat and push the needle through all four pleats from right to left. The needle will re-emerge on the left-hand side of the first pleat.

Do not pull the needle through completely. Wrap the thread around the needle six or seven times (or more if needed; this will depend on the weight of the fabric and your tension), gently place the left thumb on the coil and pull the needle through carefully.

Still holding the coiled thread, turn it over towards the right-hand side, pull the thread gently until the bullion stitch lies flat on top of the pleats and push the needle through to the back of the work. Work another one or two bullion stitches just below the first one in the same way.

One or more lazy daisy stitches (*see page 16*) may be worked on either side of the completed rose if desired.

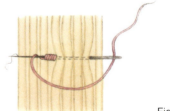

Fig. 31a

Fig. 31b

Chevron stitch (also called **Diamond stitch**) is worked from left to right. The thread is held below the needle when you work upward and above the needle when you work downward. Use the full width between two gathering threads, and work as follows:

Bring the needle up through the third pleat, just above the lower gathering thread. With the embroidery thread below the needle, pick up the next pleat. Gently pull the thread up until it rests snugly on top of the pleat.

Hold the thread below the needle and push the needle through the next pleat, just below the upper gathering thread. Gently pull the embroidery thread up.

Hold the thread above the needle and push the needle through the next pleat, also just below the upper gathering thread. Gently pull the embroidery thread down.

Hold the thread above the needle and push the needle through the next pleat, just above the lower gathering thread. Gently pull the embroidery thread down.

This completes one chevron stitch. Repeat these steps until you reach the end of the row.

Fig. 32

VARIATIONS

◆ To form diamonds, work two rows of chevron stitches opposite each other as shown in Fig. 33. If several rows are worked together, a band of diamond-shaped stitches will be formed.

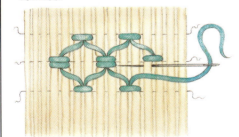

Fig. 33

◆ Another very pretty variation of the chevron stitch is a combination of chevron and cable stitches. Work as follows:

Bring the needle up through the third pleat, just above the lower gathering thread. Pick up the next pleat with the thread below the

needle, the following pleat with the thread above and the next pleat with the thread below the needle.

With the thread below the needle, push the needle through the next pleat, just below the upper gathering thread. Gently pull the embroidery thread up.

(The next three stitches are worked just below this gathering thread.) Pick up the next pleat with the thread above the needle, the following pleat with the thread below, and the pleat after that with the thread above the needle.

With the thread above the needle, pick up the next pleat, just above the lower gathering thread.

This completes one combination of the two stitches. Repeat these steps until the end of the row.

Work two rows of this combination opposite each other to form diamond-shaped stitches with little flowers between them (see Fig. 34b).

When several rows are worked to form a wide band, the effect is really lovely. The little pink dress featured on page 97 was smocked using this variation.

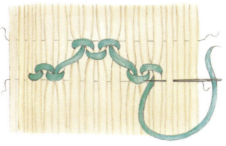

Fig. 34a

Fig. 34b

Feather stitch is worked from right to left. Use a gathering thread as a guideline. Always keep the thread below the point of the needle. Work

single feather stitch as follows: bring the needle up on the right-hand side of the third pleat, close to the gathering thread. Hold the thread down on the guideline with your left thumb. With the thread forming a circle below the guideline, make a small slanted stitch towards the guideline, picking up the third and fourth pleats. Pull the needle and thread through.

Hold the thread down on the guideline with your left thumb. With the thread forming a circle above the guideline, make a small slanted stitch towards the guideline, picking up the fourth and fifth pleats. Pull the needle and thread through.

Hold the thread down on the guideline with your left thumb. With the thread forming a circle below the guideline, make a small slanted stitch towards the guideline, picking up the fifth and sixth pleats. Pull the needle and thread through. Continue working in this manner until you reach the end of the row.

Fig. 35

Double feather stitch is worked in exactly the same way as single feather stitch, except that two stitches instead of one are worked below the guideline, and two stitches instead of one are worked above the guideline.

Fig. 36

Outline stitch is worked from left to right. From the back of the fabric, insert the needle through the third pleat. With the embroidery thread above the needle, push the needle through the next pleat, keeping the needle parallel to the gathering thread. Gently pull the embroidery thread downward until it rests snugly on top of the pleat.

Hold the thread above the needle and pick up the next pleat in the same way. Continue picking up the pleats until the end of the row.

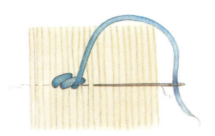

Fig. 37

For a bolder effect, work more than one row of this stitch, leaving no space between the rows.

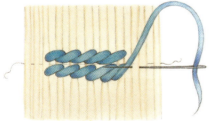

Fig. 38

Single cable stitch is worked from left to right. From the back of the fabric, insert the needle through the third pleat. Push the needle through the next pleat, with the embroidery thread below the needle. Gently pull the thread up until it rests snugly on the top of the pleat. Hold the thread above the needle and pick up the next pleat. Pull the thread down until it rests snugly on top of the pleat. Continue picking up the pleats, alternately holding the thread below and above the needle as described, until you reach the end of the row.

Fig. 39

Double cable stitch is worked in the same way as single cable, except that a second row of stitches is worked immediately below the first row, and the second row is begun with the thread held above the needle instead of below the needle. When the gathering threads are removed and the work is stretched, the double cable will look like the links of a chain.

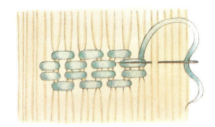

Fig. 40

Stem stitch is worked from left to right in the same way as the outline stitch, except that the thread is always held below the needle.

From the back of the fabric, insert the needle through the third pleat. With the embroidery thread below the needle, push the needle through the next pleat, keeping the needle parallel to the gathering thread. Gently pull the embroidery thread upward until the stitch you have just made rests snugly on top of the pleat. Hold the thread below the needle and pick up the next pleat. Continue until the end of the row.

If a bolder effect is required, work more than one row of this stitch, leaving no space between the rows.

Fig. 41

VARIATIONS
◆ Work one row of outline stitch (*see* above) and, just below it, one row of stem stitch, to create an interesting rope-like effect.

Fig. 42

◆ Another variation is a curved line, which creates a wave-like effect. Beginning at a gathering thread, work four stem stitches diagonally across four pleats, until you reach the next gathering thread. Curving the stitches slightly, work three stem stitches above this gathering thread. Now work four stem stitches diagonally across four pleats, down towards the first gathering thread. Curving the stitches slightly, work three stem stitches below this gathering thread. Continue in this manner until the end of the row.

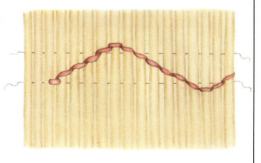

Fig. 43

Van Dyke stitch is worked from right to left, as follows: bring the needle up on the right-hand side of the third pleat, just above the lower gathering thread. With the thread below the needle, push the needle through the third and fourth pleats; then, with the thread still below the needle, push the needle through these two pleats again. This will form a back stitch over the two pleats.

With the thread still below the needle, push the needle through the fourth and fifth pleats just below the upper gathering thread and pull the thread through these two pleats. With the thread above the needle, push the needle through these two pleats again and pull the thread through.

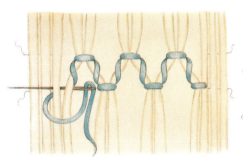

Fig. 44a

With the thread above the needle, push the needle through the fifth and sixth pleats just above the lower gathering thread and pull the thread through these two pleats. With the thread below the needle, push the needle through these two pleats again and pull the thread through. Continue in this manner until the end of the row.

Fig. 44b

Wave stitch (also called **Trellis stitch**) is worked from left to right between two gathering threads. When working upward, the thread is below the needle; when working downward the thread is above the needle. For this stitch to look neat, it is important to keep the needle parallel to the gathering threads when picking up each pleat.

Work the stitch as follows: bring the needle up through the third pleat just above the lower gathering thread. With the thread below the needle, pick up the next pleat. One at a time, pick up the next three pleats with the thread below the needle. This will bring you to just below the upper gathering thread. This completes the upward movement.

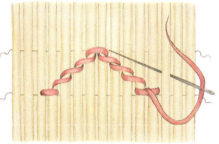

Fig. 45a

Begin the downward movement: pick up the next pleat (just below the gathering line) with the thread above the needle. One at a time, pick up the next three pleats, keeping the thread above the needle. Make sure that each downward stitch is opposite an upward stitch.

Fig. 45b

These eight stitches form one wave. Repeat until the end of the row.

More stitches may be used if you wish to create deeper waves. The idea is to pick up the same number of pleats when you work upward as you do when you work downward.

VARIATIONS
◆ To form large diamond shapes, work two rows of wave stitches opposite each other (*see* Fig. 46).

Fig. 46

◆ To form a trellis design, work several pairs of wave stitch rows, one below the other (*see* Fig. 47).

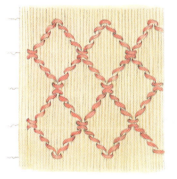

Fig. 47

SETTING THE PLEATS

It is a good idea to set the pleats after the completion of the smocking. Remove the gathering threads and put the smocked fabric on the ironing board, right side down. Stretch it slightly across the width until it is the required size and pin it to the ironing board cover; pull the pleats straight along their length. Place a damp cloth over the wrong side of the smocked fabric and *lightly* press it with a moderately hot iron. Alternatively, hold a steam iron above the fabric. Allow the smocked fabric to dry while still pinned to the ironing board and when the fabric is dry, unpin it.

· QUILTING ·

Quilting, which is the stitching together of two or three thicknesses of fabric, is a technique that has been in use for many centuries. It produces a raised effect that adds both depth and dimension to any project.

In medieval times quilted garments were worn beneath armour to protect the wearer from the cold and to prevent chafing. Beautiful quilted bedcovers were also popular because they were not only warm, but also very decorative.

Traditionally worked by hand, quilts have adorned the beds of the wealthy for many centuries and were prized possessions that were passed down from one generation to another; many beautiful examples are still to be found in homes and museums today.

There are three main types of quilting: English quilting (also known as wadded or traditional quilting), Italian or corded quilting, and Trapunto or stuffed quilting.

MATERIALS AND EQUIPMENT

FABRIC

See The Basics on page 8 for more information on fabric. Remember that all fabric to be used for quilting must be washed and ironed carefully (*see* page 8) before you begin because you cannot iron the fabric after the project has been quilted.

Backing fabric Use the same calico or fabric that you used for the front of the project. It is preferable not to use a cheaper grade of calico or fabric for the backing as the results may be disappointing.

NOTE *If you are making a cushion, which will require a separate back, you will naturally use the same fabric as for the front. This should be washed and ironed in the same way as the fabric for the front.*

Muslin For Italian quilting or Trapunto, the wadding is left out and the lining fabric used is muslin, or any other fabric with a loose weave. The design is traced on to the square of muslin, and not on to the front, and the two layers are stitched together using rows of running stitches or back stitches.

WADDING

Wadding, also known as batting, is used for English quilting and quilting candlewicked projects, and is available in various thicknesses. Be sure to use sheet wadding and not polyester stuffing, which is intended only for stuffing cushions and similar articles. For most quilted projects a thin, light-weight wadding is the most suitable and easiest to use. *See* The Basics on page 8 for information on joining wadding.

POLYESTER STUFFING

This is used in Trapunto quilting to emphasize parts of the design.

NEEDLES

Needles used for quilting should be short, sharp and strong, preferably No. 9 or No. 10 'between' needles. It is a good idea to thread several needles at once, as very often a quilting design has several rows of stitching that need to be worked on simultaneously, and this will prevent your having to stop and rethread a single needle too many times.

PINS

See The Basics, page 8.

SCISSORS

See The Basics, page 8.

THIMBLE

A thimble, which is used to push the needle through one or more layers of fabric, is absolutely essential for quilting if you want to prevent raw, punctured fingers. You will need to wear one on the middle finger of your right hand if you are right-handed (or on the middle finger of your left hand if you are left-handed). It is also sensible to wear a rubber finger-guard (turned inside out) on the index or middle finger of your other hand.

Special thimbles are available for quilting. One type is a metal thimble that has a ridge around the top and is very easy to use. Another type is made of leather and is comfortable and easy to wear if you cannot get used to a conventional thimble. Plastic quilting thimbles are also available but I find them a little uncomfortable.

QUILTING HOOP

A quilting hoop with a diameter of 30–35 cm (12–14 in), preferably mounted on a base, makes the quilting of the squares (for cushions and candlewicked quilts) much easier. Large free-standing quilting frames are available and are most useful for quilting very large projects. Unfortunately they take up a lot of space, so for the average quilter they are a little impractical. Instead, many people prefer to quilt sections of a project, such as the borders of a quilt, or even a complete project, such as a crib coverlet or cushion, without a hoop and with the work resting on a table or on their lap.

THREAD

Strong, 100 per cent pure cotton quilting thread or specially waxed quilting thread is needed. If the thread has not already been waxed, run it through a piece of beeswax to make it easier to pull through the fabric. Use 40–45 cm (16–18 in) lengths and make a knot at one end of each length.

YARN

A thick, woollen, cotton or acrylic knitting yarn or cord of a suitable thickness is used for Italian or corded quilting. It is advisable to wash pure woollen or cotton yarn in hot water before using it, to make absolutely certain that it does not shrink after the project has been completed.

PREPARING TO QUILT

> **Very important** The secret of successful quilting is tacking. Though it is a tedious job, the more tacking you do, the easier and neater the quilting will be.

1. For English quilting, trace your design on to the top fabric before tacking the three layers together. For Italian quilting and Trapunto trace the design on to the muslin backing.

2. Place the backing fabric, wrong side up, on the floor or other flat surface. If using wadding, place the wadding on top of this. Smooth out any creases in the backing or wadding. Centre the top of the project on top of the wadding.

3. Pin the three layers (or two, in the case of Italian quilting or Trapunto) together, starting from the centre and working towards the centre point of each of the outside edges. Then pin from the centre to the corners. Tack along these rows of pins. Continue to tack along radiating lines until the rows of tacking are 4–5 cm (1½–2 in) apart (*see* Fig. 48).

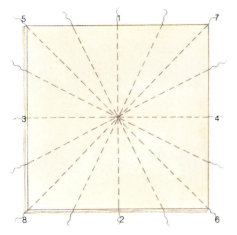

Fig. 48

On very large projects, such as quilts, it may be preferable to use the grid method of tacking. To do this, begin in the centre of the quilt and tack two parallel lines vertically towards the top of the quilt, then tack two parallel lines vertically from the centre to the bottom of the quilt. Smooth the fabric from the centre towards the outside edges and tack two lines horizontally from the centre of the quilt to the left-hand side of the quilt, then tack two lines horizontally from the centre to the

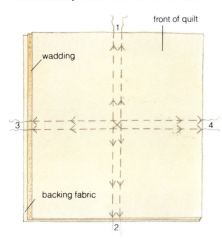

Fig. 49

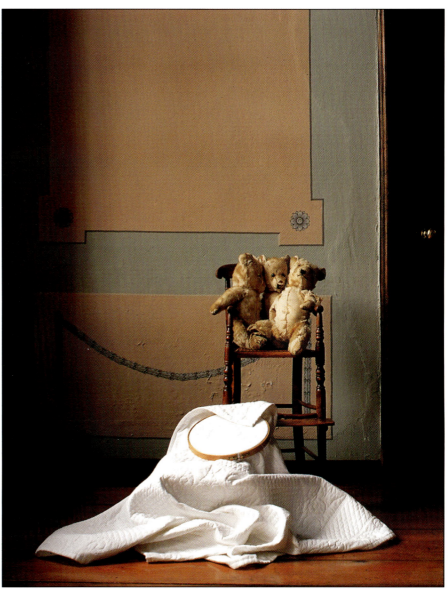

A quilted knee rug in progress.

right-hand side of the quilt. Continue working in this manner, adding more horizontal and vertical rows of tacking, 5 cm (2 in) apart, until the whole quilt has been tacked (*see* Fig. 49).

QUILTING STITCHES

Two basic stitches are used in hand quilting, whether it be English quilting, Italian or corded quilting, or Trapunto or stuffed quilting. The first

of these is running stitch, which is used for stitching together two or more layers of fabric, the top layer of which has not been embroidered or decorated in any way. The quilting stitches themselves are worked in such a manner that they provide both decoration and texture.

The second is back stitch, which is generally used for quilting around the designs on any candlewicked projects that require quilting.

It is essential that the stitches be kept small, neat and evenly spaced, both at the back and the front of the quilt. A well-quilted piece should be reversible.

Running stitch

1. Thread the needle and make a knot at one end. Work a large stitch through the top fabric and wadding, giving a little tug so that the knot is pulled through and becomes buried in the wadding. Come out at the starting point of the design.

Fig. 50a

beginning a row of quilting

2. With the thimble on the middle finger of the right hand, push the needle vertically through all three layers until it touches the middle finger of the left hand (which you have placed underneath the project). Tilt the needle quickly and, in the process, reinsert it so that it makes a small stitch at the back, and continue to push the needle up through to the front. Hold the work in place with your left thumb. The wrist of your right hand should be quite relaxed— the movement is rather like that of a see-saw as the needle is pushed in and out of the fabric. Try to put several stitches on the needle before pulling it right through the fabric.

3. To end a row of quilting, make a knot in the thread about 1 cm (½ in) from the top layer of fabric and work one back stitch, going through the wadding and coming up through the top fabric a little distance away. Tug gently and the knot will disappear into the wadding. Cut off the remaining thread.

Fig. 50b

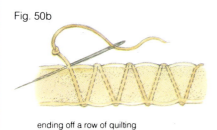

ending off a row of quilting

Back stitch

I work a back stitch beneath each French or colonial knot (an elaborate French knot) so that the quilting stitches are not visible but the quilted effect is achieved.

For this method of quilting you will need to place the fabric in a quilting hoop. Remove the outer hoop, place the project to be quilted straight down over the inner hoop, then replace and tighten the outer hoop. (The outer hoop should not be too tight and the fabric should have a little slack.) Turn the hoop upside down and check that there are no creases underneath. If there are, ease the creases away by pulling the fabric very gently. Now you are ready to begin quilting.

1. Make a knot at the end of the thread and push the needle and thread through the top fabric and wadding, coming up again under a French or colonial knot. Give the thread a little tug so that the knot is pulled through and becomes buried in the wadding (see Fig. 51).

Fig. 51

2. Place the left index or middle finger under the first French or colonial knot, pushing it up slightly. Insert the needle into the fabric just behind where the thread first emerged and push it vertically through all three (or both) layers until the needle touches the finger underneath. Tilt the needle quickly and, in the process, reinsert it so that it makes a small stitch at the back, then push it diagonally through the wadding, coming up under the next French or colonial knot. The more quickly you tilt the needle, the smaller the stitch at the back will be. Continue in this manner, working a back stitch under each knot.

3. To end the row of quilting, make a knot in the thread about 1 cm (½ in) from the top layer of fabric and work a back stitch, going through the wadding and coming up through the top fabric a little distance away. Tug gently and the knot will disappear into the wadding. Cut off the remaining thread.

QUILTING TECHNIQUES

ENGLISH QUILTING
Prepare for quilting following Steps 1–3 on pages 32–33. Quilt the design using a running stitch, following Steps 1–3 on this page.

ITALIAN OR CORDED QUILTING
1. Trace the design on to the muslin in a double line as indicated on the pattern (see Tracing the Design on to the Fabric, page 10) using a pencil or water-soluble pen.

2. Pin the square of muslin and then tack it to the back of the top layer of fabric using either of the methods described in Step 3 on page 33.

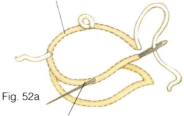

channel formed by double row of stitches

Fig. 52a

needle and yarn being pushed along the channel

3. Work small, neat running stitches (see above) along the double outline of the design and, in so doing, stitch

Fig. 52b

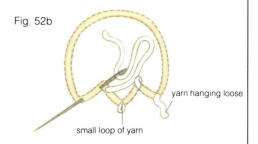

yarn hanging loose

small loop of yarn

Trapunto in progress, on reverse side (see below).

1. Trace the design on to the muslin or backing fabric (*see* Tracing the Design on to the Fabric, page 10) and tack the two pieces of fabric together using one of the methods described in Step 3 on page 33. Do not tack through the areas of the design that will be stuffed, or it will be very difficult to stuff them evenly.

2. Stitch along the lines of the design using a running stitch.

3. When the stitching is complete, decide which parts of the design you wish to accentuate. In the appropriate places, make a small hole in the muslin by pushing aside a few of the threads, and insert small pieces of polyester stuffing using a knitting needle. Make quite certain that you have pushed the stuffing into all the corners of the area and that the stuffing is evenly distributed. Move the threads back into place and secure the opening by working a few slip-stitches. For larger areas a small slit is made in the muslin, in the centre of the motif. Once you have stuffed the motif, close the slit by working a few slip-stitches.

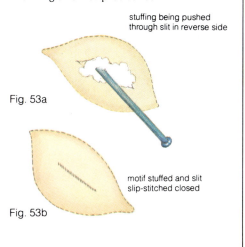

stuffing being pushed through slit in reverse side

Fig. 53a

motif stuffed and slit slip-stitched closed

Fig. 53b

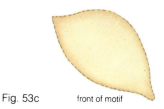

Fig. 53c   front of motif

the two layers of fabric securely together. These parallel lines of stitching form channels.

4. Thread a blunt needle or bodkin with thick, soft, woollen, cotton or acrylic yarn. Leave a short length of yarn hanging loose and, working from the wrong side, insert the needle through the muslin backing and into the channel at the beginning of a line. Push the needle and yarn along the channel until there is a bend or curve in the design. At this point, pull the needle through the muslin to the back and then reinsert it into the channel at the same point, leaving a small loop of yarn sticking out at the back. If you reach a sharp angle, do not reinsert the needle in exactly the same hole; instead, leave a small space and then reinsert the needle into the channel (leaving a small loop

of yarn) as this forms a good, neat corner. These loops will prevent the fabric from puckering should the yarn shrink. Repeat this procedure at every corner until the design is complete.

5. Leave a short length of yarn hanging loose and cut the thread.

6. Once the project is complete, remove the tacking threads.

TRAPUNTO OR STUFFED QUILTING

Very interesting effects can be created using this technique, which involves stitching two layers of fabric together, and stuffing only those areas of the design that one wishes to accentuate. The top layer of fabric should be closely woven and the backing fabric loosely woven. Muslin is quite suitable as a backing fabric.

4. Once the project is complete, remove the tacking threads.

WORKING
WITH LACE

The word 'lace' brings to mind many happy
childhood memories. I can still recall the scent of
lavender or pot-pourri that filled the air when
the linen chest was opened. Oh, how I loved
delving into this treasure chest. Inside, there
were lovely lacy sheets and pillowslips,
beautifully embroidered hand towels, magnificent
snowy-white tablecloths and handkerchiefs,
all edged with delicate lace; creamy lace collars
and cuffs and heirloom christening robes,
wrapped up in layers of tissue paper.
Lace is romantic, soft and beautiful and is also
great fun to use about the house. This can be done
in many different ways that you've probably never
thought of—all it requires is a little imagination.
Delicate lace collars and antique christening
robes or other pretty articles can be framed
and hung in almost any room.
Lace also creates a wonderful feeling of luxury.
Could anything be more relaxing than lying
among a pile of soft, sweet-smelling lace
cushions, with a good book, a cup of tea and a
big fluffy cat curled up next to you?

STORING OLD LACE

Lace should always be stored in a dry, dark place. Do not store it in plastic bags as it should be allowed to breathe. Instead, line the drawer with aluminium foil and lay the lace as flat as possible.

Never fold lace handkerchiefs or other old lace; instead, roll it up on a cardboard tube that has been covered with aluminium foil. Long lengths of lace should be treated in the same manner, as should handmade lace. Handmade lace should not be cut, but used in one piece instead.

Cover the lace with cotton fabric that has been laundered in the same way as the lace (*see* below) to protect it from dust. Moth balls should not be used because over several years the chemicals used to make moth balls could damage the lace; it is better to air the lace regularly.

PREPARING LACE FOR SEWING

It is preferable to use cotton lace rather than nylon lace to complete the projects, especially if you are using a natural fibre for the rest of the project, as the combination of a synthetic fibre and a natural fibre is not attractive.

Modern lace
Wash all modern cotton lace in very hot water or boil it in plain water for 15–20 minutes to shrink it. Place the lace in a towel and squeeze it dry. With the iron set on a moderate temperature, iron one end of the lace dry, then measure its width. On an old piece of fabric, draw two parallel lines, the distance between them being the width you have measured,

to make a template. Iron the lace lengthways using the template as a guide, to ensure an even width throughout.

Old lace
The washing process is irreversible so take great care when washing old lace or fabric, and do so only if it is in good condition. Old fibres are weaker when wet and can be damaged by too much movement, so avoid rubbing or squeezing lace when you wash it. Never starch or iron old lace. Washing agents specially designed for washing delicate lace or fabric are available; your local museum or a professional restorer should be able to recommend a reliable brand.

Alternatively, place the lace, right side uppermost, on a small piece of glass or Perspex. (It should remain on the glass or Perspex throughout the washing process.) Pre-soak the lace in plain, distilled water to remove dust and dirt; then dissolve a little pure soap in cool to lukewarm water, in a shallow container. Place the lace on the glass in the container and—with your fingers together—gently move your flattened hand up and down across the lace.

Remove the lace and the glass from the container and rinse it carefully under gently running cool to lukewarm water (a shampoo attachment works well) until the water runs clear. Distilled water should be used for the final rinse as impurities can damage the fabric.

Dry the lace on the same piece of glass. To remove the excess water, blot it gently with an old white towel (that has been laundered in the same way as the lace), and press it into shape with a flat hand. Any points at the edge of the lace may be pushed gently into place with your fingernail. It is not necessary to use pins, which may cause marking, to block the lace. Lace should always be dried away from direct sunlight.

Once the lace is quite dry, store it carefully, as described above.

SEWING LACE

All lace is slightly elastic and can therefore be stretched, so take care not to stretch it when pinning it to the fabric. If lace is stretched when it is pinned, and stitched while still stretched, the fabric will pucker when the lace returns to its original size.

LACE INSERTION
Lace insertion is a simple way to create a very pretty, delicate effect and we have used it in many of the projects in this book.

1. Pin the bottom edge of the insertion lace along the specified line. Smooth the lace upwards and pin the top edge of the lace to the fabric.

2. Tack and then machine stitch, using a straight stitch, along both long edges of the lace.

3. Working on the wrong side of the fabric, and leaving 1 cm (½ in) of fabric just inside both stitching lines, carefully cut away the excess fabric behind the insertion lace. The 1 cm (½ in) of fabric just to the inside of the stitching will then need to be made into neat hems.

4. To make the hems, turn back 5 mm (¼ in) and then a further 5 mm (¼ in) and finger-press. Pin, tack and stitch neatly by hand.

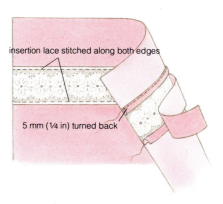

insertion lace stitched along both edges

5 mm (¼ in) turned back

Fig. 54

GATHERING LACE

Most machine-made lace has one slightly thicker thread running close to the straight edge. Find this thread and pull it gently to gather the lace quickly and easily (Fig. 55a).

If you prefer to gather the lace by machine, set the machine on the longest stitch, loosen the top tension slightly and work two rows of stitching fairly close to the straight edge of the lace (Fig. 55b). Pull both threads simultaneously and carefully gather to the required length. Reset your machine to the normal stitch length and tension.

straight edge of lace

Fig. 55a

Fig. 55b

LACE CURTAINS

Lace curtains create a soft, romantic atmosphere when used in a bedroom or sitting-room and look beautiful with sunlight filtering through the pattern of the lace or cutwork.

Curtains may be made from fairly large, lace-edged embroidered tablecloths or bedspreads. The curtains featured on page 71 are made from Battenburg lace bedspreads, which are readily available in the shops. It is advisable to leave the tablecloths or bedspreads uncut so that they may be used for their original purpose, should you wish to do so later.

Hanging lace curtains

Hang the tablecloth or bedspread over the wooden rod so that the top edge of the cloth forms a valance.

Lace curtains create a soft, romantic look in any setting.

Adjust the length so that the bottom edge of the cloth just clears the floor. Make a casing by pinning the two pieces of fabric together just below the wooden rod. Slip the cloth off the rod and tack along the line of pins, making sure that the line is straight. Stitch along this line by hand, or use a fairly long, straight machine stitch so that the row of stitches may be removed easily if desired. Slip the rod through the casing again. Remove the tacking thread, and place the rod on the brackets.

MITRING LACE

On a corner, fold the lace back on itself, with right sides together. Finger-press the fold. Fold the top

layer of lace so that its outer edge is at 90 degrees to the outer edge of the bottom layer, forming a neat corner. Finger-press the diagonal fold. Fold the lace back to the original position, with right sides together, and sew along the diagonal crease using an overlock stitch or a straight and then a zigzag stitch. Cut away the excess triangle of lace (see Fig. 56).

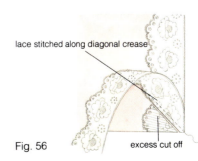

lace stitched along diagonal crease

excess cut off

Fig. 56

SEWING PROJECTS

Have you ever wondered what to do with those beautiful hand-embroidered, lace-edged tray-cloths, place-mats, handkerchiefs or table-runners? Many items in your linen cupboard may be very beautiful, but rather impractical because they are white or cream in colour. If you have too many of any of these articles, you could make them into attractive items for the home. They can be transformed into pillowslips, guest towels, cushions, nightdress cases, tablecloths or even bedspreads. This section provides clear step-by-step instructions and detailed diagrams on how to make beautiful articles from old linen and lace, and from new fabrics that are readily available in the shops today.

To avoid repeating instructions for general sewing techniques that are used throughout the projects section—and thereby to make more space available for projects—we have described these techniques below, referring back to them when necessary.

NOTE *The seam allowance for all projects is 6 mm (¼ in), unless otherwise stated.*

MAKING A PLACKET

A placket is used for the back skirt opening of a child's or baby's dress and allows the dress to be put on and removed easily. It is made before the skirt is gathered and joined to the yoke.

1. Cut a 10 cm (4 in) slit down the centre of the back section of the skirt. Cut a straight 2.5 cm x 20 cm (1 in x 8 in) strip of the same fabric to bind the slit.

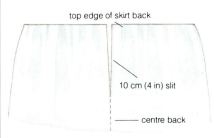

top edge of skirt back

10 cm (4 in) slit

centre back

5 mm (¼ in) seam

5 mm (¼ in) turned back along free edge of binding

binding stitched to slit in fabric (pulled straight)

Fig. 57

2. With right sides together, pin one long edge of the strip to the edge of the slit. Open the slit out into a straight line as you pin.

3. Tack and machine stitch 5 mm (¼ in) from the edge of the binding, fold back 5 mm (¼ in) to the wrong side along the other long edge of the binding, and fold the binding towards the wrong side of the fabric. Pin, tack and slip-stitch in place. Press.

MAKING AND ATTACHING A FABRIC FRILL

1. Make a narrow hem along one long edge of the frill using a narrow hemming foot (*see* page 9) or turn back 5 mm (¼ in) and a further 5 mm (¼ in). Pin, tack and machine stitch, using a straight stitch, and gather the frill using a ruffler foot (*see* page 9), or as follows: set the machine on the longest stitch, loosen the top tension slightly, and work two rows of stitching, 3–5 mm (¼ in) apart, fairly close to the raw edge of the frill (the other edge will have been hemmed). Pull both threads simultaneously and carefully gather to the required length.

An easier way to gather a frill is to draw a line on the wrong side of the fabric, parallel to, and 5 mm (¼ in) away from the unhemmed edge. Beginning at one end, and leaving a 5 cm (2 in) loose end, lay a length of strong yarn along the line, secure the loose end with a pin, and zigzag stitch over it until you reach the end. Be careful not to catch the yarn with the needle, or you will not be able to draw up the gathers easily. Leave a 5 cm (2 in) loose end and cut the yarn. Carefully draw up the gathers until the frill is the required length.

2. With right sides and raw edges together, pin it to the front of the main fabric, leaving 3 cm (1 ¼ in) of gathered frill loose at either end.

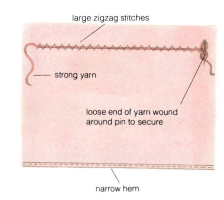

large zigzag stitches

strong yarn

loose end of yarn wound around pin to secure

narrow hem

Fig. 58a

Fig. 58b

3. Tack and then machine stitch the frill to the main fabric. Stop 2 cm (¾ in) before each corner, leaving the needle in the fabric, and raise the foot. Push as much of the raw edge of the frill as possible under the foot, lower the foot, and stitch to within 6 mm (¼ in) of the corner. Raise the foot, leaving the needle in the fabric, turn the fabric, and push as much frill under the foot as possible; lower the foot and continue. Repeat these steps at each corner, until you reach the starting point.

4. Join the two loose ends of the frill with a French seam, following the instructions given on page 43. Then machine stitch the loose fold of the frill to the fabric along the seam line that joins the frill to the front.

INSERTING A ZIP IN THE BACK OF A CUSHION COVER

1. Fold the fabric for the back section of the cushion in half vertically and finger-press. Cut along the foldline and turn back 1 cm (½ in) to the wrong side along one long side of each half.

2. Place the zipper foot on the machine and use it as a guide to keep the distance between the teeth of the zip and the machine needle constant. Place the right side of the zip uppermost, move the zipper foot to the left, and place the foldline of the left section of the back to the left of the teeth of the zip. Pin and tack, then open the zip completely. With the needle to the left of the zipper foot, machine stitch using a straight stitch (*see* Fig. 59).

3. Close the zip and place the fold of the other half of the back section next to the teeth of the zip, on the right-hand side of the zip. Move the zipper foot to the right; pin, tack and, with the needle to the right of the zipper foot, machine stitch using a straight stitch.

4. Remove the tacking threads and open the zip before sewing the back and the front of the cushion together (*see* below).

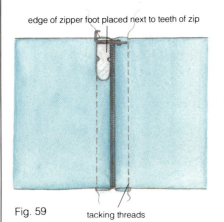

edge of zipper foot placed next to teeth of zip

Fig. 59

tacking threads

SEWING A FRENCH SEAM

The French seam is a very strong self-enclosed seam that is stitched twice—once from the wrong side and once from the right side. It is useful for sewing seams that will be visible or that will be subjected to rough treatment or frequent laundering.

Complete the seam as follows: with wrong sides together, pin and machine stitch a 5 mm (¼ in) seam. Turn the seam the other way out, so that the right sides are together, and machine stitch a slightly wider seam than the first. Press.

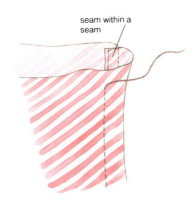

seam within a seam

Fig. 60

MITRING A CORNER

Mitring, which is the diagonal joining of two edges, is the neatest way of forming a corner. To mitre a corner, fold the fabric diagonally across the corner, on the foldline of the hem (*see* Fig. 61a). Make a crease using your fingernail.

Now open out the corner. Fold the fabric diagonally, with right sides together, and machine stitch along the crease you have made, from the fold to the turning line (*see* Fig. 61b).

Trim the seam, press open, and trim the seam allowances at the corner. Turn the hem to the wrong side and turn the edge under.

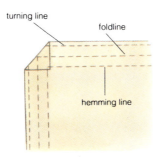

turning line

foldline

hemming line

Fig. 61a

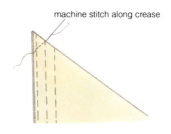

machine stitch along crease

Fig. 61b

ATTACHING CUSHION COVER FRONT TO BACK

With right sides together, and the frill pinned towards the centre, pin, tack and stitch the front to the back around all four sides using an overlock stitch or a straight and then a zigzag stitch, making sure that the zip is open.

MAKING A SEPARATE INSIDE CUSHION

Measure the cushion cover and add on 1 cm (½ in) all round. For example, if the cushion cover measures 47 cm x 47 cm (18 ½ in x 18 ½ in), the inside cushion will measure 49 cm x 49 cm (19 ½ in x 19 ½ in). Cut out two pieces of fabric (calico is usually a good choice) this size.

Pin the two pieces of calico together. Machine stitch using an overlock stitch or a straight and then a zigzag stitch around three sides. Turn right side out and press.

Stuff the cushion with polyester stuffing, pushing it right into the corners. Pin and tack the opening closed. Machine stitch using an overlock stitch or a straight and then a zigzag stitch. Trim away any ragged threads.

MAKING BUTTON LOOPS

Mark the position of the loop or loops on the edge of the garment, opposite the top and bottom of each button. Work two or three back stitches (*see* page 20) on the wrong side of the fabric. Bring the needle and thread out through the finished edge at A. Make a loop with the thread (loose enough to allow the button to pass through easily). Push the needle and thread through the fabric at B. Make several more loops of the same size. Work blanket stitch (*see* page 15) over these loops as shown in Fig. 62b, binding the loops together.

When the embroidered button loop is complete pass the needle and thread through the finished edge of the garment to the wrong side and work two or three back stitches to finish off.

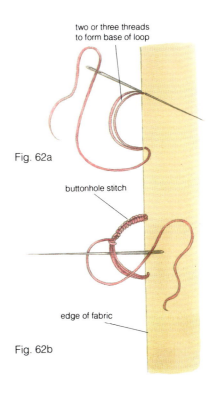

two or three threads to form base of loop

Fig. 62a

buttonhole stitch

edge of fabric

Fig. 62b

· FOR THE BEDROOM ·

Create a soft, romantic look in any bedroom by adding tucks and lace to sheets and pillowslips. Alternatively, polycotton sheeting is most suitable for making practical but pretty bed linen, and is available in many shops. Choose lace or broderie anglaise that will launder and wear well.

SHEET WITH INSERTIONS, PINTUCKS AND EMBROIDERY

If you wish to use a ready-made sheet instead of sheeting, simply unpick the wide hem of the sheet and follow the instructions below for making a decorated sheet from sheeting. It will not be necessary to sew hems along the other three edges.

Requirements
Sheeting of required size (*see* box, above) or ready-made sheet
Water-soluble pen
Matching thread
Cotton insertion lace, approximately 4 cm (1 ½ in) wide, the same measurement as the width of the sheet
Cotton edging lace of desired width, the same measurement as the width of the sheet
Satin ribbon (optional)

Making the tucks
1. Study Fig. 63 carefully. Place one raw edge of the sheeting (or the raw edge of the sheet) on a flat surface and draw lines right across the width of the sheet, parallel to, and the following distances from, the raw edge, as shown in Fig. 63, starting with line A:

Calculating the amount of fabric needed to make a sheet
Measure the width of the mattress and add twice the depth of the mattress to this measurement. Add on about 50 cm (20 in) so that the sheet can be tucked in on each side. Buy sheeting that has a width as close as possible to this measurement to avoid having to sew hems on these two sides.
    Measure the length of the mattress and add on twice the depth. Add on a 25 cm (10 in) tuck-in allowance.

LINE A: 11 CM (4 IN)

LINE B: 14.5 CM (5 ¾ IN)

LINE C: 17.5 CM (6 ¾ IN)

LINE D: 25.5 CM (10 IN)

LINE E: 29 CM (11 ½ IN)

---

2. Just above each of lines A, B, D and E (which will become the foldlines for the tucks), and 1 cm (½ in) away, draw another line. These lines (F, G, H, I) will become the stitching lines. Fold the fabric along foldlines A, B, D and E, and pin along stitching lines F, G, H and I. Tack and then machine stitch along the stitching lines, using a straight stitch.

Inserting the lace
3. Wash and iron the lace (*see* page 38). Make a narrow hem at both ends of the insertion lace by turning back 5 mm (¼ in) and then another 5 mm (¼ in) and slip-stitch. Pin the bottom edge of the insertion lace along line C. Gently smooth the lace upwards and pin the top edge of the lace to the fabric. Tack and then machine stitch, using a straight stitch, along both long edges of the lace. Complete the insertion of the lace as described on page 38.

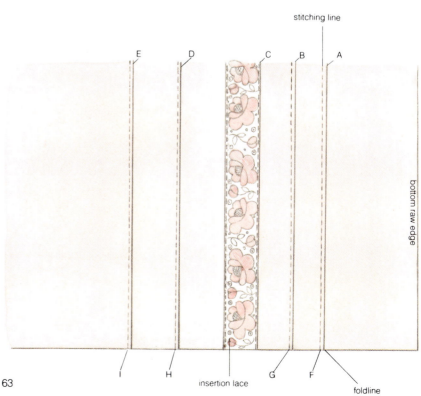

Fig. 63

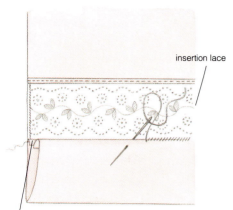

insertion lace

1 cm (½ in) seam allowance folded back and pressed away from bottom edge of insertion lace

Fig. 64

Hemming

4. Turn back 5 mm (¼ in) along the same raw edge of the sheet and then a further 6.5 cm (2 ½ in). Pin the top edge of this hem along the bottom edge of the insertion lace and tack and slip-stitch by hand.

5. Make a narrow hem at both ends of the edging lace and, with right sides together, pin the straight edge of the lace to the edge of the hem. Tack and stitch the lace in place by hand using a slip-stitch.

6. Make the hem at the other end of the sheet by turning back 1 cm (½ in) and then 2 cm (¾ in) to the wrong side. Pin, tack and machine stitch, using a straight stitch.

7. Remove the tacking threads and press the tucks so that they face away from the centre of the sheet.

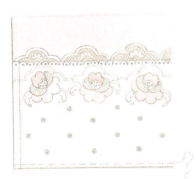

Fig. 65   straight edges of lace and hem slip-stitched together

Calculating the amount of fabric needed to make a pillowslip

We have included guidelines on how to calculate the amount of fabric required to make any pillowslip, although the projects are designed for pillows of a standard size.

Measure the width and length of the pillow and add on a 1 cm (½ in) seam allowance all round (that is, add on 2 cm [¾ in] to each measurement). Cut one piece of fabric this size. Add 2 cm to the length measurement and cut out a piece of fabric the same width, and this length, for the back. For the flap, cut a piece of fabric the same width x 20 cm (8 in).

If you are making a plain pillowslip without a frill, cut the fabric out in one piece from very wide sheeting.

Calculating the amount of fabric required for the frill

For the length, measure the perimeter of the pillow and double the measurement. Add on 1.5 cm (¾ in) for seam allowances. The width of the frill is a matter of choice, but remember to add 2.5 cm (1 in) to your chosen width for the hem of the frill and seam allowances.

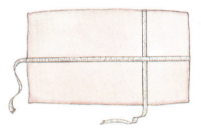

front	back	flap
front	back	flap

Fig. 66

Detail of Sheet with Insertions, Pintucks and Embroidery (page 45) showing positioning of tucks, insertion lace and edging lace.

PILLOWSLIPS TO MATCH THE SHEET

Requirements (for two pillowslips)
1.5 m (1 ⅝ yds) cotton sheeting to
  match the sheet, 200 cm (80 in)
  wide (or nearest available width)
2 m (2 ¼ yds) cotton insertion lace,
  4 cm (1 ½ in) wide
10 m (11 yds) cotton edging lace,
  2.5 cm (1 in) wide
Water-soluble pen
Matching thread

Cutting out (two pillowslips)
1. Cut the sheeting into two pieces
measuring 86 cm x 50 cm
(34 in x 20 in) for the fronts, two
pieces measuring 72 cm x 50 cm
(28 in x 20 in) for the backs, and two
pieces measuring 50 cm x 22.5 cm
(20 in x 9 in) for the flaps.

2. From the remaining sheeting, cut
five strips, each measuring 200 cm x
10 cm (80 in x 4 in), for the frills of the
pillowslips (*see* Fig. 67).

3. Wash and iron the lace (*see* page
38). Cut the insertion lace into four
equal lengths, but leave the edging
lace in one piece.

Making the tucks (one pillowslip)
4. Place one 86 cm x 50 cm
(34 in x 20 in) piece of fabric on a flat
surface and draw the following
vertical lines parallel to, and the
following distances from, the
right-hand edge, as shown in Fig. 68,
starting with line A:

LINE A: 4 CM (1 ½ IN)

LINE B: 7.5 CM (3 IN)

LINE C: 10.5 CM (4 ¼ IN)

LINE D: 18.5 CM (7 ¼ IN)

LINE E: 22 CM (8 ¾ IN)

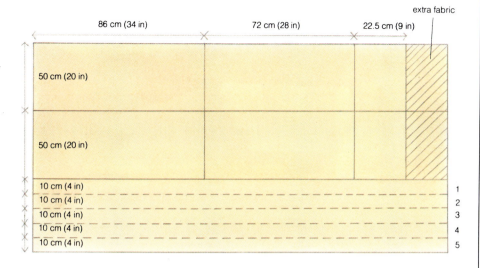

Fig. 67

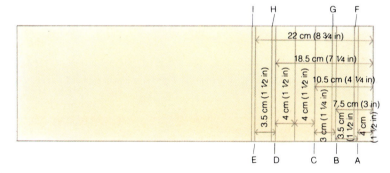

Fig. 68

5. Just to the left of each of lines A, B,
D and E (which will become the
foldlines for the tucks), and 1 cm
(½ in) away, draw another line. These
lines (F, G, H, I) will become the
stitching lines. Fold the fabric along
foldlines A, B, D and E, and pin along
stitching lines F, G, H and I. Tack and
then machine stitch along the
stitching lines using a straight stitch.

6. Remove the tacking threads and
press the tucks so that they face away
from the centre of the pillowslip.

Inserting the lace
7. Pin one edge of one length of
insertion lace along line C. Gently
smooth the lace to the left and then
pin the other edge to the fabric. Tack

and then machine stitch, using a
straight stitch, along both edges of
the lace. Complete the insertion of
the lace as described on page 38.

8. Turn the fabric around and
complete the second half of the front
of the pillowslip in exactly the same
way, following Steps 4–7.

Making and attaching the frill
9. Make a narrow hem along one long
side of each of the five strips of frill
using a narrow hemming foot (*see*
page 9), or turn back 5 mm (¼ in) and
then a further 5 mm (¼ in), and pin,
tack and machine stitch, using a
straight stitch. Then join the strips to
make one long strip using French
seams (*see* page 43).

10. Pin the wrong side of the edging lace (along its straight edge) to the hem of the frill (on the right side); then tack and machine stitch it to the frill, using a straight stitch.

11. Cut the frill into two equal lengths. Use one length of frill for this pillowslip and set the other aside for the second pillowslip.

12. Gather the frill and pin the gathered frill, with right sides and raw edges together, to the front of the pillowslip. Sew the frill to the front of the pillowslip (*see* Making and Attaching a Fabric Frill, page 42).

Attaching the flap
13. Turn under 5 mm (¼ in) and then a further 1 cm (½ in) along one long side of the fabric for the flap. Pin, tack and machine stitch. With right sides together, pin and tack the other long side of the flap to one of the short sides of the pillowslip front. Open out so that the flap lies away from the pillowslip front.

Attaching the front to the back
14. Turn under 5 mm (¼ in) and then 1.5 cm (¾ in) along one short side of the fabric for the back of the pillowslip and pin, tack and machine stitch, using a straight stitch. With right sides together, pin and tack the other three sides of the back to the front. (The frill will be sandwiched between the two layers, with the scalloped edge facing inwards.)

Completing the pillowslip
15. Fold the flap back over the back hem, and pin and tack it in place at the sides. Neatly machine stitch around the four sides of the pillowslip (being careful not to catch the hem of the back in the seam), using an overlock stitch, or a straight stitch and then a zigzag stitch.

16. Remove the tacking threads and turn the pillowslip the right way out.

PILLOWSLIPS WITH LACE INSERTIONS AND EMBROIDERY

Requirements (for two pillowslips)
1.5 m (1 ⅝ yds) cotton sheeting, 200 cm (80 in) wide (or nearest available width)
3 m (3 ¼ yds) cotton insertion lace, 4 cm (1 ½ in) wide
10 m (11 yds) cotton edging lace, 2.5 cm (1 in) wide
Water-soluble pen
Matching thread
Embroidery thread

Cutting out (two pillowslips)
1. Cut the sheeting into two pieces, each measuring 70 cm x 50 cm (27 ½ in x 20 in) for the fronts of the pillowslips, two 72 cm x 50 cm (28 in x 20 in) pieces for the backs of the pillowslips, and two 50 cm x 22.5 cm (20 x 9 in) pieces for the flaps.

2. From the remaining sheeting, cut five strips, each measuring 200 cm x 10 cm (80 in x 4 in), for the frills. (The length of each strip is the same as the width of the fabric.)

3. Wash and iron the lace (*see* page 38). Cut the insertion lace into eight equal lengths, but leave the edging lace in one piece.

Inserting the lace (one pillowslip)
4. After studying Fig. 70, place one 70 cm x 50 cm (27 ½ in x 20 in) piece of fabric on a flat surface, and draw a line diagonally across each corner in the positions marked on Fig. 70. Pin one edge of a length of insertion lace along the diagonal line in one corner so that the lace lies above the line. Gently smooth the insertion lace outwards and pin the other edge to the fabric. Tack, and then machine stitch, using a straight stitch, along both edges of the lace. Complete the insertion of the lace (*see* page 38). Insert the lace diagonally across the other three corners in exactly the same manner.

5. Embroider grub roses (*see* Bullion stitch, page 15) and leaves (*see* Lazy daisy stitch, page 16) in the positions marked on Fig. 70.

Fig. 69

Completing the pillowslip
6. Complete the pillowslip following Steps 9–16 on pages 47–48.

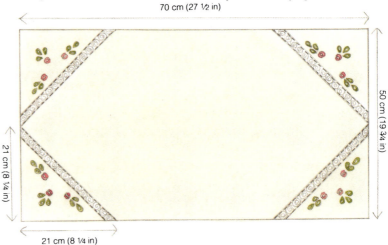

70 cm (27 ½ in)

50 cm (19 ¾ in)

21 cm (8 ¼ in)

21 cm (8 ¼ in)

Fig. 70

PILLOWSLIPS WITH WIDE INSERTION

Requirements (for two pillowslips)
1.5 m (1 ⅝ yds) cotton sheeting,
   200 cm (80 in) wide (or nearest
   available width)
Matching thread
10 m (11 yds) cotton edging lace,
   2.5 cm (1 in) wide
5 m (5 ½ yds) cotton insertion lace,
   7–9 cm (2 ¾–3 ½ in) wide
Water-soluble pen

Cutting out and making up frill
(two pillowslips)
1. Cut the cotton sheeting into two
pieces measuring 70 cm x 50 cm
(27 ½ in x 20 in) for the fronts of the
pillowslips, two pieces measuring
72 cm x 50 cm (28 in x 20 in) for the
backs of the pillowslips, and two
pieces measuring 50 cm x 22.5 cm
(20 in x 9 in) for the flaps.

2. From the remaining fabric, cut five
strips, each measuring 200 cm x
10 cm (80 in x 4 in) for the frills. (The
length of each strip is the same as the
width of the fabric.) Make a narrow
hem along one long side of each strip
using a narrow hemming foot (*see*
page 9), or turn back 5 mm (¼ in) and
then 5 mm (¼ in), and pin, tack and
machine stitch.

3. Sew the five strips together along
their short sides, using French seams
(*see* page 43) to make one long strip.
Wash and iron the lace (*see* page 38)
and then pin the wrong side of the
edging lace (along the straight edge)
to the hem of the frill (on the right
side). Tack and machine stitch, using
a straight stitch. Now cut the frill into
two halves—one for each pillowslip
—each half measuring 5 m x 10 cm
(5 ½ yds x 4 in).

4. Cut the insertion lace into two
equal lengths.

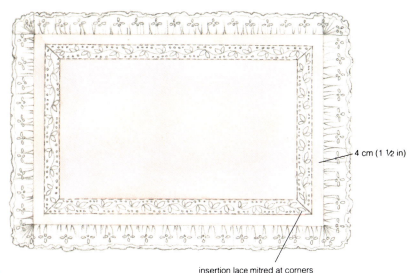

Fig. 71

4 cm (1 ½ in)

insertion lace mitred at corners

Inserting the lace (one pillowslip)
5. Place one 70 cm x 50 cm (27 ½ in x
20 in) piece of fabric on a flat surface
and draw a line 4 cm (1 ½ in) away
from, and parallel to, each of the four
edges of the pillowslip (*see* Fig. 71).
Beginning in one corner, and leaving
sufficient lace to mitre the corners
(this will be equal to the width of the
lace), pin one edge of the insertion
lace along the line, mitring the
corners as you work (*see* page 39).

6. Gently smooth the lace towards the
centre of the pillowslip, and pin the
other edge to the fabric. Tack and
then machine stitch along both edges
of the lace, using a straight stitch.
Complete the insertion of the lace by
cutting away the fabric behind the
lace and hemming (*see* page 38).

Completing the pillowslip
7. Complete the pillowslip following
Steps 9–16 on pages 47–48.

FROM LEFT TO RIGHT: *Pillowslip to Match the Sheet* (*page 47*) *and Pillowslip with Lace Insertions and Embroidery* (*page 48*).

QUILTED BED COVER

This quilt fits a standard double bed and measures 200 cm x 250 cm (80 in x 100 in). For making quilts for beds of other sizes refer to Determining the Overall Dimensions of the Quilt (Steps 1 and 2) on page 54.

Use soft polyester/cotton sheeting or two standard double-bed polyester/cotton sheets to make this quilt. The fabric should not be too tightly woven because fabric with a very tight weave is difficult to quilt. Light-weight wadding (no more than 1 cm [½ in] thick) is easier to quilt than thick wadding.

Requirements
Tracing paper
5 m (5 ½ yds) polyester/cotton
    sheeting, 200 cm (80 in) wide
    (or nearest available width), or two
    double-bed sheets (hems unpicked)
Water-soluble pen
205 cm x 255 cm (81 in x 100 ¾ in)
    wadding (*see* information on
    joining, page 8)
Saucer or other round object
Strong tacking thread
Strong quilting thread
1 m (1 ⅛ yds) matching fabric,
    200 cm (80 in) wide, for making the
    binding (*see* box, page 51)

Cutting out
1. Cut the sheeting into two equal halves, each measuring 2.5 m x 200 cm (2 ¾ yds x 80 in) and spread one half on a large, flat surface. Set the other half aside for the backing.

2. Working from the left, make a series of accurate, corresponding marks at the top and bottom of the fabric to divide it into nine equal panels, each 21 cm (8 ¼ in) wide, with a 1 cm (½ in) space between panels (*see* Fig. 72). After marking the top and bottom edges, join the marks with vertical lines. Divide each panel in half

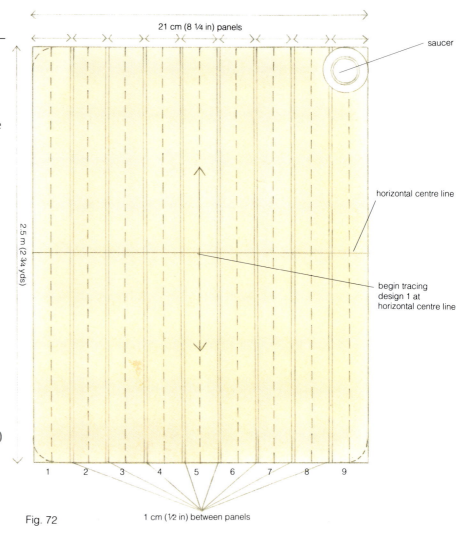

Fig. 72

vertically again and draw a line; this will be the centre line of each panel.

Tracing the designs
3. Fold the fabric in half horizontally and draw a line across the centre to create the horizontal centre line.

4. Trace the quilting designs on pages 113 and 114 on to tracing paper. Matching the vertical centre lines of design and panel, trace quilting design 1 (page 113) on to panel 5, beginning at the horizontal centre line and working towards the bottom edge of the panel. Then trace the same design on to the upper half of panel 5, beginning at the horizontal centre line and working towards the top edge of the panel.

5. Working in exactly the same way as you did on panel 5, and always working from the centre panel (panel 5) outwards, trace quilting design 1 on to panels 3, 7, 1 and 9; and quilting design 2 (page 114) on to panels 4, 6, 2 and 8.

Preparing to quilt
6. After tracing the designs on to the panels, place the backing fabric on the floor, place the wadding on top of it and then lay the quilt front (traced designs uppermost) on top of the wadding. Straighten out any creases in the three layers before you start to pin. Pin the three layers together, beginning in the centre of the quilt and working out to the centre of the outside edges using either of the

methods described in Step 3 of Preparing to Quilt on page 33.

7. Place a round saucer on one of the corners of the quilt and trace around one side of it to round off the corner of the quilt; round off the other three corners in the same way. Stay-stitch and then cut away the excess fabric.

8. Tack the three layers together along the pinned lines; tack until the rows are no more than the width of a hand apart at the outside edges.

Quilting
9. Begin quilting at the horizontal centre line of panel 5 and work towards the edge of the quilt (*see English Quilting, page 34*). Turn the quilt around and complete the second half of panel 5 in the same way. Starting at the centre line every time and working as you did on panel 5, quilt the remaining panels in the following order: 4, 6, 3, 7, 2, 8, 1 and 9. Remember to quilt the vertical, parallel lines between the panels.

10. Once all the quilting is complete, trim away any excess wadding so that all three layers are the same size. Tack around the perimeter of the quilt, fairly close to the edge.

Binding
11. Beginning in an inconspicuous place, bind the edges of the quilt as follows: with right sides and raw edges together, pin one long edge of the strip of binding (*see box, right*) to the edge of the quilt, easing the binding as you pin around the corners until you reach the starting point. Join the two short ends together and press the seam open. To complete the binding, follow Step 3 of Making a Placket on page 42, but do not press.

Completing the quilt
12. Remove all the tacking threads and erase the marks made by the water-soluble pen by dabbing the lines with a damp sponge or cloth.

The Quilted Bed Cover (page 50) can also be put to good use in an outdoor setting.

Making continuous binding
If a long strip of bias binding is required it is best to make a continuous strip, as follows:

Cut a rectangle of fabric on the straight grain. Decide on the width of the bias strip and cut a long piece of cardboard the same width. Fold the top right-hand corner of the fabric down to meet the opposite long side of the rectangle (*see Fig. 73a*). Hold the corner down and finger-press along the crease. Open the fabric out and turn it over to the wrong side. Draw a line along the crease using a long ruler. Use the long cardboard marker to mark and draw as many lines (parallel to the first one) as are required to make up a bias strip of the desired length. Referring to Fig. 73b, cut along the two cutting lines, discarding the remaining fabric. With right sides together, fold the rectangle to form a tube so that the following lines meet: A and B; C and D, as shown in Fig. 73c. Pin and machine stitch a seam. Iron the seam open and cut in a continuous line, beginning at C and finishing at B.

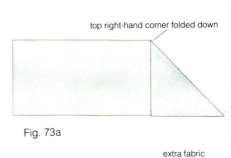

top right-hand corner folded down

Fig. 73a

extra fabric

cutting line

cutting line

extra fabric

Fig. 73b

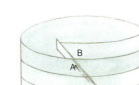
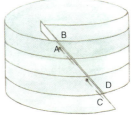

Fig. 73c

MEASUREMENT CHARTS

These charts provide measurements for quilts for various conventional bed sizes. Readers are advised to work to either metric or Imperial measurements (which have been rounded up to the nearest half- or quarter-inch), and not to use a combination of the two.

QUILTS WITH SASHING

SINGLE-BED QUILT (12 Squares)

QUILT SIZE		No. of squares	x	Size of squares	+	No. of sashings	x	Width of sashings	+	No. of borders	x	Width of borders
Width	181 cm (71 in)	3	x	37 cm (14 ½ in)	+	2	x	10 cm (4 in)	+	2	x	25 cm (10 in)
Length	228 cm (90 in)	4	x	37 cm (14 ½ in)	+	3	x	10 cm (4 in)	+	2	x	25 cm (10 in)
Width	190 cm (75 in)	3	x	40 cm (16 in)	+	2	x	10 cm (4 in)	+	2	x	25 cm (10 in)
Length	240 cm (96 in)	4	x	40 cm (16 in)	+	3	x	10 cm (4 in)	+	2	x	25 cm (10 in)

SINGLE-BED QUILT (15 Squares)

Width	160 cm (63 ½ in)	3	x	30 cm (12 in)	+	2	x	10 cm (4 in)	+	2	x	25 cm (10 in)
Length	240 cm (96 in)	5	x	30 cm (12 in)	+	4	x	10 cm (4 in)	+	2	x	25 cm (10 in)
Width	165 cm (65 ¼ in)	3	x	35 cm (14 in)	+	2	x	10 cm (4 in)	+	2	x	20 cm (8 in)
Length	255 cm (100 ¾ in)	5	x	35 cm (14 in)	+	4	x	10 cm (4 in)	+	2	x	20 cm (8 in)

DOUBLE-BED QUILT (12 Squares)

Width	195 cm (76 in)	3	x	45 cm (18 in)	+	2	x	10 cm (4 in)	+	2	x	20 cm (8 in)
Length	250 cm (98 in)	4	x	45 cm (18 in)	+	3	x	10 cm (4 in)	+	2	x	20 cm (8 in)
Width	200 cm (80 in)	3	x	40 cm (16 in)	+	2	x	10 cm (4 in)	+	2	x	30 cm (12 in)
Length	250 cm (100 in)	4	x	40 cm (16 in)	+	3	x	10 cm (4 in)	+	2	x	30 cm (12 in)

QUEEN-SIZE BED QUILT (16 Squares)

Width	250 cm (100 in)	4	x	45 cm (18 in)	+	3	x	10 cm (4 in)	+	2	x	20 cm (8 in)
Length	250 cm (100 in)	4	x	45 cm (18 in)	+	3	x	10 cm (4 in)	+	2	x	20 cm (8 in)
Width	250 cm (100 in)	4	x	40 cm (16 in)	+	3	x	10 cm (4 in)	+	2	x	30 cm (12 in)
Length	250 cm (100 in)	4	x	40 cm (16 in)	+	3	x	10 cm (4 in)	+	2	x	30 cm (12 in)

KING-SIZE BED QUILT (16 Squares)

QUILT SIZE	No. of squares	x	Size of squares	+	No. of sashings	x	Width of sashings	+	No. of borders	x	Width of borders
Width 260 cm (102 in)	4	x	45 cm (18 in)	+	3	x	10 cm (4 in)	+	2	x	25 cm (10 in)
Length 260 cm (102 in)	4	x	45 cm (18 in)	+	3	x	10 cm (4 in)	+	2	x	25 cm (10 in)

QUILTS WITHOUT SASHING

SINGLE-BED QUILT (15 Squares)

QUILT SIZE	No. of squares	x	Size of squares		+		No. of borders	x	Width of borders
Width 165 cm (65 ¼ in)	3	x	35 cm (14 in)		+		2	x	30 cm (12 in)
Length 235 cm (92 ¾ in)	5	x	35 cm (14 in)		+		2	x	30 cm (12 in)
Width 170 cm (67 ½ in)	3	x	40 cm (16 in)		+		2	x	25 cm (10 in)
Length 250 cm (100 in)	5	x	40 cm (16 in)		+		2	x	25 cm (10 in)

DOUBLE-BED QUILT (12 Squares)

	No.	x	Size		+		No.	x	Width
Width 204 cm (81 in)	3	x	48 cm (19 in)		+		2	x	30 cm (12 in)
Length 252 cm (100 in)	4	x	48 cm (19 in)		+		2	x	30 cm (12 in)
Width 200 cm (80 in)	3	x	50 cm (20 in)		+		2	x	25 cm (10 in)
Length 250 cm (100 in)	4	x	50 cm (20 in)		+		2	x	25 cm (10 in)

QUEEN-SIZE BED QUILT (20 Squares)

	No.	x	Size		+		No.	x	Width
Width 220 cm (86 in)	4	x	40 cm (16 in)		+		2	x	30 cm (12 in)
Length 260 cm (102 in)	5	x	40 cm (16 in)		+		2	x	30 cm (12 in)
Width 220 cm (86 in)	4	x	45 cm (18 in)		+		2	x	20 cm (8 in)
Length 265 cm (104 in)	5	x	45 cm (18 in)		+		2	x	20 cm (8 in)

KING-SIZE BED QUILT (16 Squares)

	No.	x	Size		+		No.	x	Width
Width 260 cm (102 in)	4	x	50 cm (20 in)		+		2	x	30 cm (12 in)
Length 260 cm (102 in)	4	x	50 cm (20 in)		+		2	x	30 cm (12 in)

CANDLEWICKED QUILTS

Candlewicked quilts—and any other quilts made up of blocks—can be made in one of two ways. The traditional method involves framing each candlewicked square individually with lace and joining the squares with horizontal and vertical sashing between them. Using the simpler method, all the squares are sewn together, without any sashing between them, and the lace is sewn on top of the seams.

Before beginning work on your quilt, read the general instructions and those for the two methods of assembling a candlewicked quilt, which are described in detail on the next few pages, very carefully. The method you choose will determine the size of the squares to be cut—in order to accommodate the sashing, the squares for a traditional quilt will, naturally, be smaller than those for a quilt without sashing.

Determining the overall dimensions of the quilt

Before working out the number and size of the squares, you will need to determine the exact dimensions of the quilt for your particular bed. To do this you will need to measure the mattress:

1. Measure the width of the mattress and add twice the depth of the mattress to this measurement. Add on an extra 30 cm (12 in) to allow for an overhang of 15 cm (6 in) on either side of the mattress.

2. Measure the length of the mattress and add twice the depth of the mattress to this measurement. Add an extra 15 cm (6 in) to allow for an overhang at the foot of the bed.

NOTE *As one normally uses a valance around the base of the bed the quilt needs to hang only 15 cm (6 in) below the bottom of the mattress, and on three sides of the bed only, not at the top.*

If your bed has both a footboard and a headboard, it will not be necessary to add 15 cm (6 in) to the length measurement.

CONVENTIONAL BED SIZES

To determine the size and number of squares you require for your quilt, consult the tables (pages 52–53) for quilts with and without sashing. The calculations are based on the measurements of a modern sprung mattress with a depth of about 18 cm (7 in) and cover many of the popular mattress sizes.

UNCONVENTIONAL BED SIZES

You may find that the measurements of your mattress and, therefore, the size of your quilt, do not correspond with those given in the tables on pages 52–53.

If this is the case, refer to the tables and select the quilt size closest to the one you require. It is preferable to choose a quilt that is too large rather than too small for your bed. However, you may wish to calculate the size of the squares yourself—a process that will involve a certain amount of trial and error. It will be difficult to achieve exactly your desired width and length, as one determines the other, so you need to decide which is the more critical, and be flexible about the other. (*See* page 55.)

CUTTING OUT SQUARES, BORDERS AND SASHING

Before cutting out the squares, add 2 cm (¾ in) to the length and width measurements of each. For example, if the measurement of the square is 45 cm x 45 cm (18 in x 18 in), the size of the square you will cut out will be 47 cm x 47 cm (18 ½ in x 18 ½ in). This extra 2 cm (¾ in) includes a 6 mm (¼ in) seam allowance and allows for shrinking and puckering of the fabric.

At a later stage, once you have completed the candlewicking, the squares will be washed and then blocked (cut exactly square).

Add an extra 2 cm (¾ in) to the width of each border. If using the traditional method, add on the extra 2 cm (¾ in) to the width of each piece of sashing.

Fig. 74

15 cm (6 in)

15 cm (6 in)

15 cm (6 in)

mattress depth

Determining the size of the squares for a quilt with sashing

There are four measurements that you will require when making a quilt with sashing, namely, size of squares, number of squares across the width, width of borders, and width of sashings. You will have to decide on three of these, and will then be able to calculate the fourth.

In the following example, the desired overall width of the quilt is 230 cm (90 ½ in) and the length is 265 cm (104 in), and it has been decided that the width is the more critical. The border width, number of squares across the width and the width of the sashings have been established, and the size of the squares must be calculated.

Border width: 15 cm (6 in)
Sashing width: 10 cm (4 in)
No. of squares across width of quilt: 6

Step 1 Subtract twice the width of the border from the overall width:
    230 cm (90 ½ in)– (2 x 15 cm |6 in|) = 200 cm (80 in)

Step 2 From this figure, subtract five times the width of the sashing (there will be five lots of sashing if there are six squares across the width):
    200 cm (80 in) – (5 x 10) = 150 cm (60 in)

Step 3 Divide the remaining width by the number of squares across the width:
    150 cm (60 in) ÷ 6 = 25 cm (10 in)

The squares are to measure 25 cm x 25 cm (10 in x 10 in).

Now you can determine the length of your quilt, bearing in mind that the border width, sashing width and square size must remain the same. Because the desired length is 265 cm (104 in), you will require one more square than across the width, which measures 230 cm (90 ½ in).

Calculations for a quilt with seven squares down its length:

Step 1 Multiply the number of squares by the length of one square:
    7 x 25 cm (10 in) = 175 cm (69 in)

Step 2 To this figure, add twice the width of the border:
    175 cm (69 in) + (2 x 15 cm |6 in|) = 205 cm (81 in)

Step 3 Now add six times the width of the sashing (there will be six lots of sashing if there are seven squares down the length):
    205 cm (81 in) + (6 x 10 cm |4 in|) = 265 cm (104 in)

The finished length of this quilt will be 265 cm (104 in), which, as it happens, is the length originally intended. You could, however, arrive at a length longer or shorter than originally intended. In this case you may want to rework the calculations, adjusting one or more of the variables, until you arrive at a more acceptable figure.

For a quilt without sashing, there are only three variables to be considered, namely, size of squares, number of squares, and width of borders.

NOTE *Remember to add 2 cm (¾ in) to the width and length measurements of each square, and an extra 2 cm (¾ in) to the width measurement of each border before cutting them out.*

A quilt makes a comfortable 'rug' for a picnic.

QUILT WITH SASHING

Requirements (for a 200 cm x 250 cm [80 in x 100 in] quilt)
10 m (11 yds) calico, 150 cm (60 in) wide or 12 m (13 yds) calico, 120 cm (48 in) wide for the squares, sashing, borders and backing
20–22 m (21 ½–24 yds) cotton lace, 7 cm (2 ¾ in) wide
Water-soluble pen
Embroidery hoop
Crochet cotton or embroidery thread
Graph paper
Matching thread
214 cm x 264 cm (84 in x 104 in) thin wadding (*see* information on joining wadding, page 8)
Quilting thread

Preparing and cutting out the fabric
1. Wash and iron the fabric for the quilt (*see* page 8) and the lace (*see* page 38).

2. Measure the mattress (*see* page 54). Refer to the measurement charts (pages 52–53) and select the appropriate quilt size for your bed or, if your bed is not a conventional size, calculate the size and number of squares you need (*see* page 55). Remember to add 2 cm (¾ in) to all the measurements given to allow for shrinkage and puckering. A 6 mm (¼ in) seam allowance is included.

3. Cut out the fabric required for the sashing and borders of your quilt and then the squares. Cut the vertical sashing and all the borders approximately 5 cm (2 in) longer than the finished length and width of the quilt. Cut the horizontal sashing the full width of the fabric; do not cut it into short lengths yet.

NOTE *It is always a good idea to pull a thread instead of tearing the fabric, as tearing will stretch the edges and make assembling the quilt more difficult.*

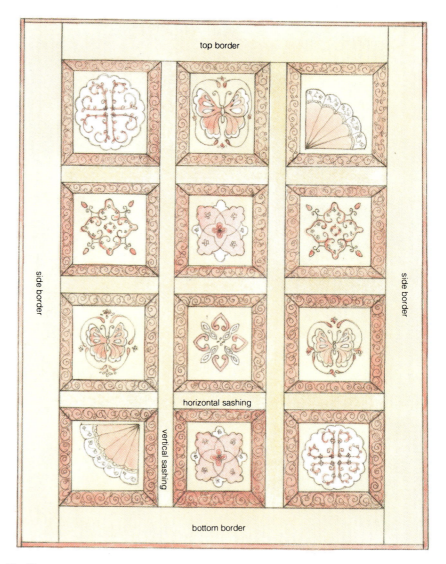

Fig. 75

Tracing the designs
4. Trace the required number of designs (pages 118–137) on to the squares, centring them accurately (*see* page 10). Any inaccuracy will be apparent once the quilt is complete.

NOTE *Accuracy is most important at all stages of making a quilt, as it will save you a great deal of time and effort when you assemble your quilt.*

Candlewicking
5. Place a calico square in the hoop, and pull the fabric taut.

6. Select the threads you enjoyed using on your sampler (*see* page 10) and candlewick the designs.

7. When you have candlewicked all the squares, wash them all, together with the fabric for the sashing and the borders, in soapy water. Wash each square very carefully, making sure that you remove the ring marks that the hoop might have made, as well as any other dirty marks.
   Rinse all fabric thoroughly in plain, cold water and then use fabric softener in the usual way.

NOTE *It is very important that the squares and the fabric for the borders and sashing are washed together, and that all dirty marks are removed during this wash. If any of the fabric needs to be washed a second time, it will become a shade lighter than the rest. This will spoil the overall look of your quilt.*

8. Wrap each square individually in a towel and squeeze dry. Do the same for the fabric for the sashing and borders. *Do not* hang out to dry.

9. Place a thick towel (not an embossed one) folded double, on the ironing board. Put each square, candlewicked side down, on the towel and iron it carefully. Too hot an iron might scorch the fabric.

10. Iron the sashing and borders lengthways to ensure an even width throughout.

Blocking the squares

11. The tension of your work and the ironing may have altered the original size and shape of the squares and it is important that they are all the same size. Measure each square vertically and horizontally along the centre lines to determine which is the smallest. Use graph paper to make an accurate template, the sides of which are the same length as the shortest side of the smallest square. Paste this template on to fairly stiff cardboard and cut it out carefully.

12. Find and mark with a water-soluble pen the centre point of each of the sides of the template and of each fabric square.

13. Place each fabric square, in turn, on a smooth table surface. *Do not* stretch the edges of the fabric square, even if the thread has shrunk and pulled the square out of alignment. Smooth the edges and stick the fabric square to the table with tape. Place the template on top of the fabric, line up the centre points of the template with those of the square, draw round the edges of the template, and trim the fabric down to this size. Your candlewicked squares should now all be perfectly square and the same size.

14. Lay the horizontal sashing on the table and, using the same template as before, mark and then cut the sashing into short pieces the same length as one side of a square (the number of pieces will depend on the size of the quilt). These short pieces will be sewn between the squares.

Attaching the lace to the squares

15. Cut four pieces of lace for each square, each the same length as one side of a square. (Use the template you used to block the squares and short sashing.) Make sure that the pattern of the lace is balanced at both ends (that is, that it doesn't stop halfway through the pattern on one side and not on the other).

16. Pin, tack and sew the lace to the top and bottom of each square and then to the sides, stitching 2–3 mm (⅛ in) in from the raw edge of the square and again 2–3 mm (⅛ in) in from the inner edge of each strip of lace. Neatly tack the ends of the lace to the edges of the fabric. Complete all the squares in the same way.

17. Trace the quilting designs on to all the short pieces of horizontal sashing, beginning at the centre point of each piece and working out towards the edges, before you assemble the quilt.

Assembling the quilt

18. Lay out the completed squares in the desired positions.

19. Beginning with panel 1, match the bottom corners of the first square with the top corners of a piece of horizontal sashing, and with right sides together, pin the sashing to the square, working your way from the centre to the corners. Ease, tack and then stitch, using the foot of your sewing machine as a guide. (In this way, you can make sure that the row of stitching on the lace will not be visible, as it will be sewn to the inside of the seam.)

20. Pin, tack and stitch the top edge of the next square to the bottom edge of the sashing. Continue in this manner until you have sewn the first panel of four squares. Now assemble the second panel of four squares and then the third in the same way. You will now have three panels, each consisting of four squares.

21. To strengthen the seams, overlock them, or use another row of straight stitching and then a zigzag stitch. Press all the seams so that they lie towards the squares.

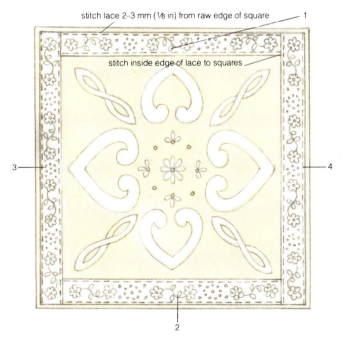

stitch lace 2–3 mm (⅛ in) from raw edge of square   1

stitch inside edge of lace to squares

3

4

2

Fig. 76

Fig. 77

22. Trace a quilting design on to both pieces of vertical sashing, as described in Step 17.

NOTE *Following the next few instructions carefully is extremely important as it will make all the difference as to whether all the corners line up accurately or not.*

23. Measure the distance between where the sewing machine needle enters the fabric when using a straight stitch and the raw edge of the square. This measurement will be about 6 mm (1/4 in), depending on the make of your machine, and will be the seam allowance for all your seams.

24. Draw this 6 mm (1/4 in) seam allowance right across the top end of each piece of vertical sashing and the first square of each of the three panels. Take the measurement from the 6 mm (1/4 in) mark at the top left-hand corner of the first square to the bottom left-hand corner of the

same square. Take another measurement from the bottom left-hand corner of the first square to the bottom left-hand corner of the first strip of horizontal sashing. Mark these measurements on a long strip of paper. Now, starting from the 6 mm (1/4 in) mark at the top end of the vertical sashing, mark off these two measurements all the way down both sides of both pieces of vertical sashing (*see* Fig. 78).

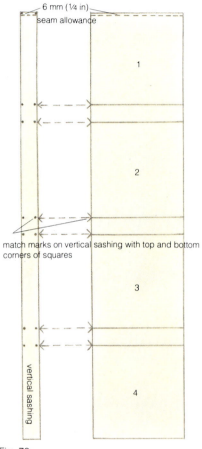

Fig. 78

25. Matching these marks with the corners of the squares, and with right sides together, pin the two pieces of vertical sashing to the three panels (so that they lie between the panels). Tack and machine stitch using an overlock stitch, or a straight stitch and then a zigzag stitch.

26. Measure the front of the quilt across the width and trim the top and bottom borders to this length. Measure the length of the quilt; include the width of the top and

bottom borders and trim the side borders to this length.

27. Trace a quilting design on to the four border pieces, beginning at the centre point of each border and working out towards the corners. This will ensure that the design is balanced at both ends.

28. With right sides together, pin, tack and machine stitch the borders to the squares, beginning with the top and bottom borders and then going on to do the sides. Overlock these seams, or strengthen them using a straight stitch and then a zigzag stitch.

29. Give the completed front of the quilt a final pressing. Do not press the borders with a steam iron if you have used a water-soluble pen to trace the quilting design as any steam or water will erase the design.

Attaching the wadding and backing fabric
30. Measure the completed quilt front and cut the wadding and backing fabric 5–7 cm (2–2 3/4 in) wider than the front of the quilt on all four sides. (You will therefore add 10–14 cm [4–5 1/2 in] to the length and 10–14 cm [4–5 1/2 in] to the width.)

31. Place the backing fabric on the floor (wrong side uppermost), centre the wadding over it, and smooth it out. Now lay the quilt front (candlewicked side uppermost) on top of the wadding. Make quite sure that you straighten out any creases in all the layers before you start to pin.

32. Carefully pin all three layers together (you may need the help of a friend to do this), beginning in the centre and working your way out towards the centre of the outside edges, using either of the methods described in Step 3 on page 33.

33. Using a strong thread, tack the three layers together.

The candlewicked Quilt with Sashing (page 56) is used as a bedspread, while the Quilted Bed Cover (page 50) is folded at the foot of the bed. Of special interest is the use of lace at the head and foot of the bed.

NOTE *The more you tack, the easier it will be to quilt, as tacking prevents the wadding from shifting too much.*

Quilting

34. Quilt the twelve candlewicked squares using a back stitch, starting from the centre of the quilt and working your way towards the outside edges and corners (*see* page 34 for instructions on quilting). Smooth any excess fullness towards the edges as you work.

NOTE *When quilting the sashings and the borders, start at the centre point of each piece and work towards the corners or edges.*

35. Quilt the horizontal and vertical sashing, and finally, the borders.

36. Once you have completed the quilting of the borders, trim the excess wadding to the same size as the quilt front, leaving the backing 4 cm (1 ½ in) wider all around. Tack around the perimeter of the quilt and

fold the edges of the protruding backing in half (towards the wadding) and press.

37. Now fold this folded edge over the edges of the quilt front to create a self-binding. Begin with the top and bottom edges and then do the side edges. Pin, tack and slip-stitch into place. To make sure that the wadding is held firmly in place, quilt close to the hem that has just been made. Remove all the tacking threads.

QUILT WITHOUT SASHING

This method is much quicker and easier than the first method and is far more suitable for a beginner. Whether you use the first or second method, however, you are sure to be delighted with the finished quilt. As mentioned before, it will be necessary to make the squares proportionately larger to make up for the lack of sashing.

Requirements (for a 204 cm x 252 cm [81 in x 100 in]) quilt
10 m (11 yds) calico, 150 cm (60 in) wide or 12 m (13 yds) calico, 120 cm (48 in) wide for squares, borders and backing
About 16 m (18 yds) cotton lace, 5–9 cm (2–3 ½ in) wide
Water-soluble pen
Embroidery hoop
Crochet cotton or embroidery thread
Graph paper
Stiff cardboard
Matching thread
218 cm x 266 cm (86 in x 104 in) thin wadding (*see* information on joining wadding, page 8)
Strong tacking thread
Quilting thread

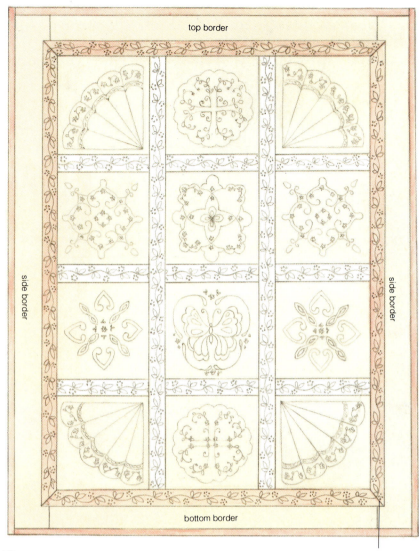

Fig. 79

Preparing and cutting out the fabric
1. Wash and iron the fabric (*see* page 8) and the lace (*see* page 38).

2. Measure the mattress, following the instructions on page 54. Refer to the table of quilt measurements on pages 52–53 and select the quilt size appropriate to your bed. Add on an extra 2 cm (¾ in) to all the measurements given to allow for shrinkage and puckering. A 6 mm (¼ in) seam allowance is included.

3. Cut the borders approximately 5 cm (2 in) longer than the finished width and length of the quilt. Cut out the number of squares required for your quilt.

NOTE *Always pull a thread instead of tearing the fabric, as tearing will stretch the edges, making it more difficult to cut out the squares accurately and to assemble the quilt.*

Tracing the designs
4. Trace the designs (pages 118–137) on to the squares, centring accurately (*see* page 10). Any inaccuracy will be apparent once the quilt is complete.

Candlewicking
5. Place each calico square in the hoop, in turn, and pull the fabric taut.

6. Candlewick the designs (*see* pages 20–21) using the desired threads.

7. After you have candlewicked all the squares, wash them all with the fabric for the borders and backing, in soapy water. Wash each square very carefully, making sure that you remove the marks that the hoop might have made, and any other dirty marks. Rinse all the fabric in plain water and then use fabric softener in the usual way.

NOTE *It is very important that all dirty marks are removed during this wash. If any of the fabric needs to be washed a second time, it will become a shade lighter than the rest of the fabric and this will spoil the overall look of your quilt.*

8. Wrap each square individually in a towel and squeeze dry. Do the same for the fabric for the borders. Do *not* hang the fabric out to dry as the creases will be difficult to remove.

9. Place a thick towel (not an embossed one), folded double, on the ironing board. Put each square, candlewicked side down, on the towel and iron it carefully. Be careful not to use too hot an iron as it might scorch the fabric.

10. Iron the borders lengthways to ensure that the width of the border remains the same throughout.

Blocking the squares

11. The tension of your work and the ironing may have altered the original size of your squares and it is important that they are all cut to the same size.

Measure each square horizontally and vertically along the centre lines to determine which is the smallest. Use graph paper to make an accurate template, the sides of which are the same length as the shortest side of the smallest square. Paste this template on to the cardboard and cut it out carefully. By using this template you can ensure that all the squares will be the same size.

12. Find and mark the centre point of the sides of the template and of each fabric square with a water-soluble pen.

13. Place each fabric square, in turn, on a smooth table surface. Do not stretch the edges of the fabric, even if the thread has shrunk and pulled the square out of alignment. Smooth the edges and stick the fabric square to the table with tape. Place the template on top of the fabric, line up the centre points of the template with those of the square, draw around the edges of the template and trim the fabric down to size.

Your squares should now all be perfectly square and the same size.

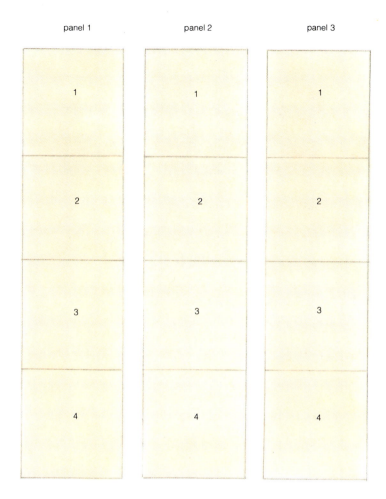

Fig. 80

Assembling the quilt

14. Lay out the squares in position. With right sides together, stitch the squares together in three panels of four squares each, as shown in Fig. 80. Overlock the seams, or strengthen them using a straight and then a zigzag stitch, and press them so that they all lie in the same direction.

15. With right sides together and corners matching, tack and stitch panel 1 to panel 2 and panel 2 to panel 3 (*see* Fig. 80). Overlock the seams or use a straight and then a zigzag stitch, and press.

16. Measure the front of the quilt across the width and trim the top and bottom borders to this length. Measure the length of the quilt, including the width of the top and bottom borders, and trim the side borders to this length.

Attaching the lace and the borders

17. Cut three lengths of lace a little longer than the width of the quilt (before the borders are sewn on), making sure that the pattern is balanced at both ends of the lace. Match the centre lines of the lace with the three horizontal seam lines and pin the lace to the fabric (*see* Fig. 81). Tack and stitch into place along both edges of the lace.

18. Cut two lengths of lace a little longer than the length of the quilt (before the borders are sewn on), again making sure that the pattern is balanced at both ends of the lace. Match the centre lines of the lace with the two vertical seam lines and pin the lace to the fabric (*see* Fig. 81). Tack and stitch into place.

19. Tack the raw ends of the lace to the edges of the fabric.

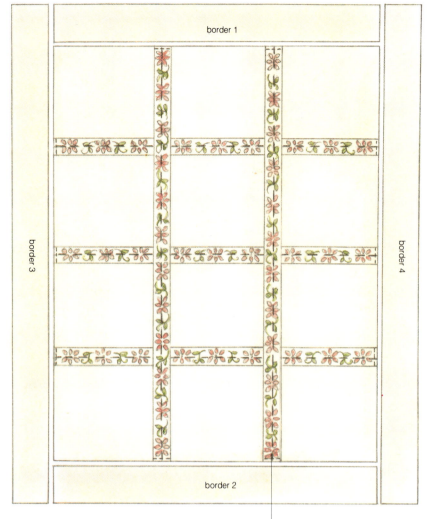

border 1

border 3

border 4

border 2

centre line of lace positioned over seam lines

Fig. 81a

20. With right sides together, pin, tack and machine stitch the top and bottom borders and then the two side borders to the quilt using an overlock stitch or a straight and then a zigzag stitch. Trim away any excess fabric and then press.

21. Pin the lace that frames the entire central section of the quilt in the position shown in Fig. 79. Mitre the corners (*see* page 39), tack, and stitch into place.

22. Using a water-soluble pen, trace the quilting designs on to the four borders, beginning in the centre of each border and working your way out, towards the corners.

Attaching the wadding and backing fabric

23. Measure the completed quilt front and cut the wadding and backing fabric 5–7 cm (2–2 ¾ in) wider than the quilt front on all four sides. (In other words, you will add 10–14 cm |4–5 ½ in| to the length, and 10–14 cm |4–5 ½ in| to the width.)

24. Place the backing fabric on the floor (with the wrong side uppermost), centre the wadding over it and smooth it out. Now lay the completed quilt front (candlewicked side uppermost) on top of the wadding. Make absolutely sure that you straighten out any creases in all three layers before you start to pin.

25. Carefully pin the three layers together (you may need the help of a friend to do this), beginning in the centre and working your way out towards the centre of the outside edges using either of the methods described in Step 3 on page 33.

26. Using a strong thread, tack the three layers together.

NOTE *The more you tack, the easier it will be to quilt as tacking prevents the wadding from shifting too much.*

27. Quilt the twelve candlewicked squares using a back stitch, starting from the centre of the quilt and working your way towards the outside edges and corners (*see* page 34 for instructions on quilting). Smooth any excess fullness towards the edges as you work.

28. Quilt the borders, beginning the quilting at the centre point of each border and working towards the corners. Once you have completed the quilting of the borders, trim the excess wadding so that it is the same size as the quilt front, leaving the backing 4 cm (1 ½ in) wider all the way round. Tack around the perimeter of the quilt and fold the edges of the protruding backing in half (towards the wadding) and press.

29. Now fold the folded edge over the quilt front to create a self-binding. Begin with the top and bottom edges and then do the side edges. Pin, tack and slip-stitch into place. To ensure that the wadding is held firmly in place, quilt close to the hem that has been made. Remove tacking threads.

folded edge of binding folded over quilt front and pinned

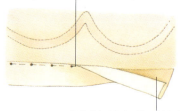

Fig. 81b   4 cm (1 ½ in) wide backing folded in half

CUSHION COVER WITH PINTUCKS, RIBBON AND LACE

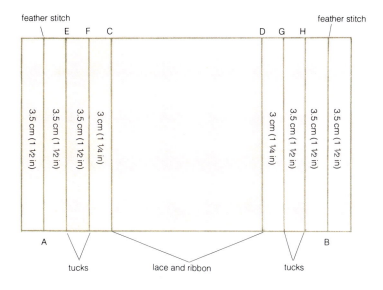

Fig. 82

Requirements

Water-soluble pen
33 cm x 45 cm (13 in x 18 in) piece of fabric for the front
Embroidery thread
Matching thread
66 cm (26 in) cotton edging lace, 2.5 cm (1 in) wide
66 cm (26 in) satin ribbon, 1 cm (½ in) wide
3.5 m (3 ⅞ yds) fabric for the frill, 10 cm (4 in) wide
42 cm x 33 cm (16 ½ in x 13 in) piece of fabric for the back
35 cm (14 in) zip

Embroidery and tucks

1. Study Fig. 82 carefully and, using a water-soluble pen, draw vertical lines in the positions marked on the fabric for the front. Now work a row of feather stitches (see page 15) along lines A and B.

2. Form the tucks along lines E, F, G and H as follows: make a fold along line E and finger-press, then place the edge of the machine foot on the edge of the fold and stitch, using a straight stitch. Sew the tucks along lines F, G and H in the same manner. Place a damp cloth over the tucks and press them so that they lie flat and face outwards.

Attaching the lace and ribbon

3. Cut the edging lace in two and pin the straight edge of one of the strips to line C, so that the scalloped edge faces outwards. Tack and machine stitch using a straight stitch, very close to the straight edge of the lace.

4. Cut the satin ribbon into two equal lengths and pin one length along the straight edge of the lace, so that the

edge of the ribbon overlaps the straight edge of the lace and hides the stitching. Tack and machine stitch, using a straight stitch, along both edges of the ribbon.

5. Pin, tack and sew the second strip of lace and then the second length of ribbon to line D. Stitch the ends of the strips of lace and ribbon to the edges of the fabric.

Gathering and attaching the frill

6. Make a narrow hem along one long edge of the fabric for the frill, using a narrow hemming foot (see page 9) or fold back 5 mm (¼ in) and then another 5 mm (¼ in) and stitch using a straight stitch. Gather the frill, and, with right sides and raw edges together, pin the frill to the cushion front, leaving 3 cm (1 ¼ in) of gathered frill loose at each end. Tack and machine stitch the frill to the cushion front (see Making and Attaching a Fabric Frill, page 42).

Inserting the zip and completing the cushion cover

7. Insert the zip in the fabric for the back (see page 42). Attach the fabric for the back to the front (see page 43).

8. Make an inside cushion to fit (see page 43).

LACY HANDKERCHIEF CUSHION COVER

You may have several handkerchiefs that you never use, but wish you could find a use for, put away in a drawer. This beautiful, dainty cushion is made from a handkerchief.

Requirements

Embroidered square handkerchief (not smaller than 28 cm x 28 cm [11 in x 11 in])
Fine cotton lawn for the back of the cushion
2.5–3 m (2 ¾–3 ¼ yds) cotton edging lace, 9 cm (3 ½ in) wide
Matching thread
Zip, at least 3 cm (1 ¼ in) longer than the back of the cushion

Measuring and cutting out

1. Measure the width of the handkerchief; add 2 cm (¾ in) to this measurement and cut a piece of lawn for the back of the cushion, using the new width measurement and the same length measurement as the handkerchief. For example, if the handkerchief is 28 cm x 28 cm (11 in x 11 in), cut a piece of fabric measuring 30 cm x 28 cm (12 in x 11 in).

Attaching the lace

2. Gather the cotton edging lace (*see* page 39) and pin it, right sides and raw edges together, to the cushion front. Leave 3 cm (1 ¼ in) of gathered lace at each end. Tack and machine stitch the lace to the cushion front, close to the edges (*see* Making and Attaching a Fabric Frill, page 42).

Inserting the zip and completing the cushion cover

3. Insert the zip in the fabric for the back of the cushion cover, following the instructions on page 42.

4. Complete the cushion cover by attaching the front to the back, remembering to keep the zip open (*see* page 43). Make an inside cushion to fit (*see* page 43).

LACE CUSHION COVER

This lace cushion cover is a reproduction of a Victorian cushion cover, and is very feminine and pretty.

Requirements

Graph paper

1.38 m (1 ½ yds) cotton insertion lace, 5 cm (2 in) wide

1.2 m (1 ¼ yds) cotton insertion lace, 2.5 cm (1 in) wide

Matching thread

1.5 m (1 ⅝ yds) cotton insertion lace, 3 cm (1 ¼ in) wide

3.5 m (3 ⅞ yds) cotton edging lace, 9 cm (3 ½ in) wide

33 cm x 48 cm (13 in x 19 in) fine cotton lawn for the back of the cushion

4 pearl buttons

Raymond the cat lies comfortably against the Lacy Handkerchief Cushion (page 63). Behind are the Lace Cushion (this page) and the Cushion with Pintucks, Ribbon and Lace (page 63).

Making the template

1. To make an accurate template, mark out a 27 cm x 32 cm (10 ½ in x 12 ½ in) rectangle on a larger piece of graph paper.

Positioning the lace

2. Referring to Fig. 83a, place the first broad strip of 5 cm (2 in) wide insertion lace diagonally across the centre of the template, right side up, leaving 1 cm (½ in) extra at both ends. Pin the lace to the paper template and cut the lace. Then place the 2.5 cm (1 in) wide lace next to the first strip, again leaving 1 cm (½ in) extra at both ends. Pin and cut the lace. Continue alternating the broad and narrow lace in this manner until you have completely covered the template.

Joining the lace

3. Carefully slip-stitch the strips of lace together, and then stay-stitch around the outline of the rectangle (through the lace and the paper). Neaten the edges of this rectangular panel by leaving about 3 mm (⅛ in) of the lace and trimming away all excess lace.

Attaching the border of lace

4. Starting and finishing at the top left-hand corner, and leaving 4 cm (1 ½ in) extra at both ends, pin the 3 cm (1 ¼ in) wide insertion lace (right side up) to the edge of the centre panel, along all four sides, carefully mitring the corners (*see* page 39). When you reach the top left-hand corner again, carefully mitre the fourth corner. The edge of the border must overlap the centre panel by about 2 mm (⅛ in). Tack and then remove the paper template. Stitch the border to the centre panel by hand, using tiny running stitches.

Attaching the lace frill

5. Gather the cotton edging lace (*see* page 39) and pin it, right sides and raw edges together, to the outer edge of the cushion front (to the border you

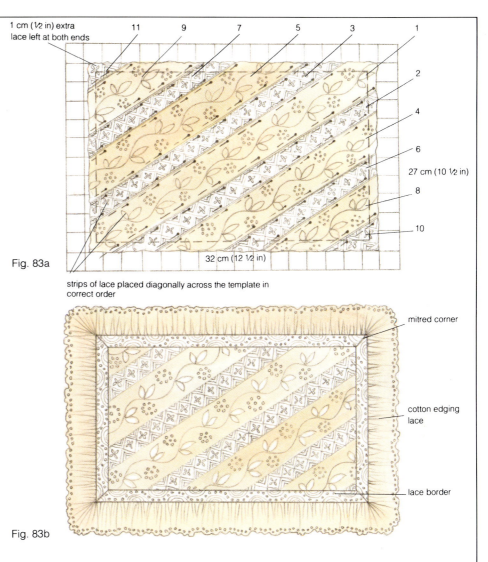

Fig. 83a

strips of lace placed diagonally across the template in correct order

Fig. 83b

mitred corner

cotton edging lace

lace border

have attached). Leave 3 cm (1 ¼ in) of gathered lace loose at either end. Machine stitch the edge of the gathered lace to the cushion front, close to the raw edge (*see* Making and Attaching a Fabric Frill, page 42).

6. When you reach the starting point, join the two ends of the lace together using a French seam (*see* page 43). Machine stitch the loose fold formed by the French seam to the back of the frill along the seam line that joins the front of the cushion to the frill.

Attaching the buttons and completing the cushion cover

7. Cut the 33 cm x 48 cm (13 in x 19 in) fine cotton lawn for the back of the cushion cover into two sections: section A, to measure 18 cm x 33 cm (7 in x 13 in), and section B, 30 cm x 33 cm (12 in x 13 in). Along one side of section A, turn 1 cm (½ in) to the

wrong side, and then a further 1 cm (½ in). Pin, tack and machine stitch, using a straight stitch.

8. Along one long side of section B, turn back 3 cm (1 ¼ in) and then a further 3 cm (1 ¼ in). Pin, tack and stitch using a straight stitch.

9. Sew the four buttons close to the edge of the hem on section A, spacing them evenly.

10. On section B, make four buttonholes to correspond with the buttons. Fasten the buttons, and pin the sections together, between the buttons and buttonholes, so that the openings do not gape.

11. Complete the cushion cover by attaching the front to the back (*see* page 43). Make an inside cushion to fit (*see* page 43).

CANDLEWICKED CUSHION

Requirements
Tracing paper
Water-soluble pen
33 cm x 36 cm (13 in x 14 in) piece of
    fabric for front
Embroidery hoop
Crochet cotton or embroidery thread
68 cm double-edged eyelet lace
Matching thread
3.75 m (4 yds) fabric for the frill,
    10 cm (4 in) wide
33 cm x 38 cm (13 in x 15 in) piece of
    fabric for back
35 cm (14 in) zip

Candlewicking
1. Trace the design on page 140 on to tracing paper.

2. Trace the design on to the fabric in the positions indicated in Fig. 84a using the water-soluble pen.

3. Place the fabric in the hoop and pull taut. Using crochet cotton or embroidery thread, candlewick the design and, when complete, wash and iron the fabric carefully (see page 8).

Attaching the lace
4. Cut the double-edged eyelet lace into two strips, each measuring 34 cm (13 ½ in). Place the strips of lace in the positions shown in Fig. 84b. Pin the lace to the fabric, then tack and machine stitch, using a straight stitch, close to both edges of each strip of lace. Sew the raw ends of the lace to the edge of the fabric.

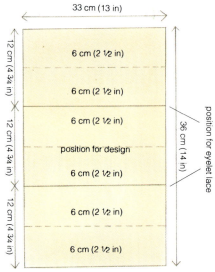

Fig. 84a

Gathering and attaching the frill
5. Make a narrow hem along one long edge of the frill, gather the frill and attach it to the cushion front following the instructions on page 42.

Inserting the zip and completing the cushion cover
6. Insert the zip in the fabric for the back of the cushion (see page 42).

7. Complete the cushion cover by attaching the front to the back of the cushion (see page 43) and make an inside cushion to fit (see page 43).

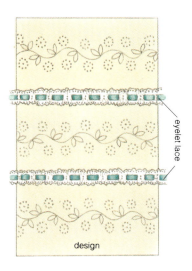

Fig. 84b

NIGHTDRESS CASE

Requirements
Tracing paper
43 cm x 74 cm (17 in x 29 in) white
    cotton or linen fabric (cut to 37 cm
    x 68 cm [14 ½ in x 27 in] once the
    embroidery is complete; see Step 1,
    below)
Water-soluble pen
Embroidery hoop
Embroidery thread
Matching thread
92 cm (36 in) white cotton lace or
    broderie anglaise, 2.5 cm (1 in) wide

A Victorian Nightdress Case (this page), finely embroidered in shades of pink, adds a touch of colour to a bedroom decorated in white.

Embroidery

1. Select a design from pages 137–139 and trace it on to tracing paper. After washing and ironing the fabric as described on page 8, trace the design on to the flap of the nightdress case using the water-soluble pen. (If the fabric is cut to the finished size before the embroidery is completed, it will be too small to fit into the embroidery hoop.)

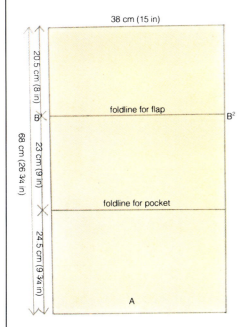

Fig. 85a

2. Complete the embroidery and wash and iron the fabric carefully (*see* page 14).

Hemming

3. Cut the fabric to the correct size. Make a hem along the bottom edge (A) of the fabric (*see* Fig. 85a), by turning back 5 mm (¼ in) and then 1 cm (½ in). Pin, tack and machine stitch, using a straight stitch. Make a narrow hem at the top edge by turning back 5 mm (¼ in) and then another 5 mm (¼ in). Make narrow hems along both sides of the top flap (between the top edge and B¹ and B²) by turning back 5 mm (¼ in) and then another 5 mm (¼ in). Pin, tack and machine stitch, using a straight stitch.

Attaching the lace

4. Carefully wash and iron the cotton lace (*see* page 38).

Fig. 85b

5. Make a narrow hem (to the wrong side) on both short ends of the cotton lace. Pin the lace to the front of the flap, beginning at B¹ and ending at B² and mitring the corners (*see* page 39). Tack and then machine stitch close to the straight edge of the lace using a straight stitch.

Completing the nightdress case

6. With wrong sides together, fold the bottom hem (A) up to B and pin the corners at B¹ and B² (*see* Fig. 85a).

7. Join the front to the back along both side edges, using French seams (*see* page 43), allowing 4 mm (¼ in) for the first seam and 6 mm (¼ in) for the second. Turn the nightdress case the right way out and press carefully, using a damp cloth.

Fig. 85c

VARIATION

If you have more embroidered or lace-edged place-mats or tray-cloths than you need, you can put one of them to good use by making this nightdress case.

Requirements

1 tray-cloth or place-mat
Linen fabric to match, for the pocket section (*see* Steps 2 and 3, below)
Matching thread

Cutting out

1. Cut the tray-cloth or place-mat in half across the width, so that it measures approximately 22 cm (8 ¾ in) in depth (*see* Fig. 86). This piece will be used to make the flap of the nightdress case.

2. Match the fabric of the cloth as closely as possible to another piece of fabric. (If the tray-cloth or place-mat is white linen or cotton, use an old linen or cotton sheet, or buy a piece of cotton or linen fabric of a suitable weight.)

3. Bleach the cut cloth and the linen fabric together, rinse carefully and iron dry. Measure one long side of the cut tray-cloth. Cut out the fabric for the pocket section; it should be approximately the width of the cut cloth plus 2 cm (¾ in) and 48 cm (19 in) in length (*see* Fig. 86).

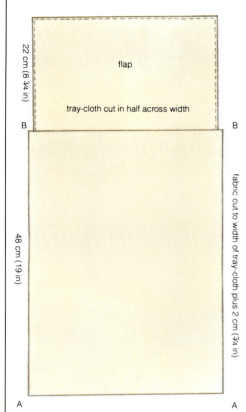

flap

tray-cloth cut in half across width

22 cm (8 ¾ in)

48 cm (19 in)

fabric cut to width of tray-cloth plus 2 cm (¾ in)

B — B

A — A

Fig. 86

Attaching front to back

4. Sew one long side of the cut cloth to one short side of the matching linen or cotton fabric using a French seam (*see* page 43).

5. Make a hem at the bottom edge (A) of the fabric by turning back 5 mm (¼ in) and then a further 1 cm (½ in). Pin, tack and machine stitch using a straight stitch.

Completing the side seams

6. With wrong sides together, fold the bottom hem up to B and pin the corners at B, as shown in Fig. 85c. Pin, tack and then sew the two side seams using a straight stitch and a seam allowance of 4 mm (¼ in). Turn the nightdress case inside out and, with the right sides together, pin, tack and machine stitch a 6 mm (¼ in) seam using a straight stitch. These French seams will not be visible as they will be on the inside of the completed nightdress case.

Turn the right way out, remove all the tacking threads and press carefully using a damp cloth.

CANDLEWICKED MIRROR SURROUND

Requirements

Tracing paper
50 cm x 45 cm (20 in x 18 in) piece of white cotton or linen fabric
Water-soluble pen
Embroidery hoop
Crochet cotton or embroidery thread
1.3 m (1 ½ yds) white cotton lace, 1.5 cm (⅝ in) wide
Matching thread
28 cm x 22 cm (11 in x 8 ¾ in) piece of white cotton or linen fabric for the facing
43 cm x 37 cm (17 in x 14 ½ in) stiff cardboard
All-purpose glue
43 cm x 37 cm (17 in x 14 ½ in) foam rubber, 1 cm (½ in) thick
Sharp blade
Pegs
Mirror (without a frame) to cover oval opening (*see* page 141)

Candlewicking

1. Trace the pattern and the design on page 141 on to tracing paper.

2. Fold the 50 cm x 45 cm (20 in x 18 in) fabric in half horizontally, and then vertically, and finger-press. Matching the centre lines of the fabric and the design, trace the design on to the fabric.

3. Tack along the oval line of the design so that when the fabric is washed, you will still be able to see where the opening will be.

4. Place the fabric in a hoop and candlewick the design. Wash and iron the completed design very well (*see* page 14).

Gathering and attaching the lace

5. Wash and iron the cotton lace (*see* page 38). Gather the lace (*see* page 39) and pull up the gathers to fit the oval.

Join the ends of the lace using a very narrow French seam (*see* page 43), an overlock stitch, or a straight stitch and then a zigzag stitch, and press the seam flat.

6. With right sides together, and the scalloped edge of the lace facing outwards, pin the lace (along the gathering line) to the fabric, along the oval line (*see* Fig. 87a) and tack. Remove the pins.

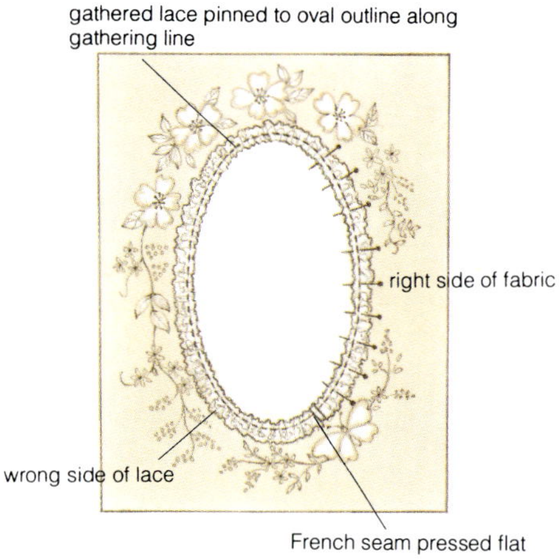

gathered lace pinned to oval outline along gathering line

right side of fabric

wrong side of lace

French seam pressed flat

Fig. 87a

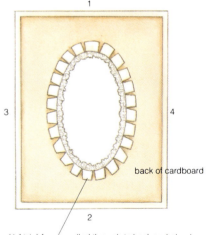

3 cm (1 ¼ in) facing pulled through to back and glued to cardboard

back of cardboard

Fig. 87b

7. Pin the linen or cotton fabric for the facing to the front of the candlewicked fabric. On the wrong side of the candlewicked fabric, tack all three layers (that is, the front, the lace and the facing) together along the oval line. Now machine stitch along this line, using an overlock stitch, or a straight stitch and then a zigzag stitch. Cut away the fabric within the oval, being careful not to cut any of the machine stitches. Leaving the facing about 3 cm (1 ¼ in) wide all the way around the opening, carefully cut off the excess fabric.

Attaching front to backing

8. Trace the oval on to the wrong side of the cardboard, making sure that it is properly centred. Turn the cardboard over, glue the piece of foam rubber to the cardboard and press it down firmly. Turn the cardboard to the wrong side again, and use a sharp blade to cut along the oval line, right through the cardboard and the foam rubber. Discard the inner oval.

9. Remove the tacking threads, and pull the facing through the opening to the back of the cardboard, until the stitching line sits snugly on the edge of the opening. The lace will now form a frill around the edge of the opening. Glue the wrong side of the facing securely to the back of the cardboard. Leave to dry, and then gently smooth the candlewicked fabric towards the outer edges of the cardboard. Secure with pegs. Beginning at the top edge, fold the excess fabric towards the back of the cardboard and glue securely, using the pegs to hold the fabric firmly until the glue dries. Next, fold back and glue the bottom edge, and then the two sides. Make the folds as neat as possible, although the corners and edges will be covered by a wooden frame. Remove pegs.

10. Stick the back of the cardboard to the front of the mirror around the edges, making sure that the entire opening is covered. Frame the mirror and surround, using a purchased picture frame, or have it framed professionally.

Candlewicked Mirror Surround (page 68) worked in a variety of stitches and coloured thread.

DOUBLE FABRIC RUFFLE FOR ROUND MIRROR

Double Fabric Ruffle for Round Mirror (*this page*).

Requirements

2 strips of fabric 7.5 cm x 1.5 m
  (3 in x 1 ⅝ yds)
2 strips of fabric 10 cm x 1.5 m (4 in x
  1 ⅝ yds)
Matching thread
6 m (6 ½ yds) cotton edging lace,
  1–2.5 cm (½–1 in) wide
6 m (6 ½ yds) satin ribbon, 1 cm
  (½ in) wide
Water-soluble pen
Ball of strong yarn
All-purpose glue
1 round mirror 29 cm (11 ½ in) in
  diameter
1 strip of fabric 10 cm x 1.5 m (4 in x
  1 ⅝ yds) for a bow (optional)

Hemming

1. Make a narrow hem along *both* long sides of the two narrower (7.5 cm [3 in]) strips of fabric, using a narrow hemming foot (*see* page 9). Alternatively, turn back 3–4 mm (⅛–¼ in) and then a further 5 mm (¼ in) to the wrong side and pin, tack and stitch using a straight stitch.

2. Make a narrow hem along only one long side of both of the wider (10 cm [4 in]) strips of fabric. (If you make a hem on the other side of these strips, the gathers will become too bulky and the top frill will not lie correctly.) Overlock the other long side of both of these strips of fabric, or use a straight and then a zigzag stitch.

Joining the strips

3. Sew the two narrower strips of fabric together, using a French seam (*see* page 43), so that they form one long strip of fabric. Do the same with the two wider strips of fabric.

Attaching the lace

4. Wash and iron the cotton lace (*see* page 38) and cut it into two equal

lengths. On the right side of the fabric, pin the straight edge of one of the pieces of lace (with the right side uppermost and the scallops facing outwards) to the outer edge of the narrower strip of fabric. Tack and machine stitch, using a straight stitch. Sew the second piece of lace to the outer edge of the wider strip of fabric in the same way.

Attaching the ribbon

5. Cut the ribbon into two equal lengths. Pin one of the lengths of ribbon along the straight edge of the first piece of lace, so that the edge of the ribbon overlaps the lace, and hides the stitching. Tack, then slowly machine stitch with a straight stitch along both edges of the ribbon. Stitch the second piece of ribbon to the wider strip of fabric in exactly the same way.

Joining the remaining sides of the strips

6. On the wrong side of the narrower strip of fabric, draw a line parallel to, and 1 cm (½ in) away from, the edge that doesn't have the lace sewn to it (this will be the inner edge) with a water-soluble pen. Do likewise with the wider frill.

7. Join the two remaining short sides of the narrower strip of fabric, using a French seam (*see* page 43), being careful to align the lace and ribbon correctly. Join the two remaining short sides of the wider strip of fabric in the same way.

Gathering the ruffles

8. Beginning at one of the seams, and leaving a 5 cm (2 in) loose end, lay the yarn along the line, secure the loose end with a pin, and zigzag stitch over it until you reach the same seam. Be careful not to catch the yarn with the needle, or you will not be able to draw up the gathers easily. Leave a 5 cm (2 in) loose end and cut the yarn and threads. Do the same with the wider circle of fabric.

9. Measure the circumference of the mirror, and draw up the gathers of the wider fabric circle to fit this measurement, forming the outer ruffle. Secure the loose ends of the yarn well, and adjust the gathers.

Attaching the ruffles to the mirror

10. Apply the glue to the right side of the mirror in a line around the extreme outer edge. Apply the glue in a line to the wrong side of the wider, outer ruffle along the gathering line. Allow the glue to become 'tacky', then firmly press the wrong side of the fabric to the right side of the mirror. If necessary, re-adjust the gathers of the ruffle to fit the circumference of the mirror. Press the gathers firmly to the mirror a second time.

11. Measure the new, smaller, circumference and draw up the gathers of the narrower circle of fabric to fit, forming the inner ruffle. Secure the loose ends of the yarn very well, and adjust the gathers. Attach this ruffle to the mirror, following the same procedure as before.

Making the bow

12. Cut the short ends of the remaining piece of fabric at a slant. Using a narrow hemming foot (*see* page 9), make a hem along the outside edges of the fabric, or turn back 5 mm (¼ in) and then a further 5 mm (¼ in) and pin, tack and stitch using a straight stitch. Tie it into a pretty bow and, positioning it carefully, glue it to the inner ruffle.

LACY TIFFANY LAMPSHADE

This beautiful lampshade matches the curtains on page 39, the Round Ruffled Tablecloth on page 79, the Cushion with Pintucks, Ribbon and Lace on page 63, and the Lace Cushion on page 64. With a fitted lining and a loose cover, it is simple to make and looks most effective.

Requirements

37 cm (14 ½ in) white cotton fabric, 115 cm (45 in) wide, for the lining
Matching thread
Tiffany lampshade frame, 35 cm (14 in) in diameter
Narrow elastic
90 cm x 90 cm (35 ½ in x 35 ½ in) white lace or lace-edged tablecloth

Making the lining

1. Join the short sides of the fabric using a French seam (*see* page 43). Press the seam flat.

2. Make a casing along both the top and the bottom edges by turning 5 mm (¼ in) and then 1 cm (½ in) to the wrong side. Pin, tack and machine stitch using a straight stitch, leaving an opening in both casings so that the elastic may be threaded through.

3. Place the lining over the lampshade frame so that the top casing is in line with the top metal ring of the frame. Thread the elastic through the casing and pull it up so that the top edge of the lining is the same size as the metal ring. Cut the elastic and sew the two ends together by hand to secure. Neatly stitch the opening closed by hand.

4. Without removing the lining from the lampshade, thread the elastic through the lower casing and pull the elastic fairly tight. (The balance of the fabric will cover the lower metal ring of the frame, and will be pulled

Lace Curtains (*page 39*), Lacy Tiffany Lampshade (*this page*), lace tablecloth, Round Ruffled Tablecloth (*page 79*) and heart-shaped Dried Flower Wreath (*variation, page 109*).

towards the inside of the opening by the elastic.) Pin the two ends of the elastic together, stitch securely by hand, and cut off the remaining elastic. Stitch the opening closed.

Fitting the cover

5. Find the centre point of the cloth or lace by folding it in half horizontally and then vertically. Finger-press.

6. Measure the diameter of the top circle of the lampshade frame (*see* Fig. 88). Using a compass, and placing it on the centre of the cloth, draw a circle with the same diameter.

7. Carefully cut away the fabric within the circle and bind the hole using an overlock stitch or bias binding (*see* Making a Placket, page 42).

measure diameter

Fig. 88

8. Place the lampshade cover over the frame and the lining and pass the light fitting (without the bulb) through the central opening. Replace the bulb.

·FOR THE BATHROOM·

HAND TOWEL

Good quality, medium-weight linen or pure cotton, or pieces of old white sheets, are quite suitable for making hand towels, as all these fabrics are very absorbent.

Requirements (for one generous-sized hand towel)
Water-soluble pen
90 cm x 70 cm (35 ½ in x 27 ½ in) fabric for the towel
70 cm (27 ½ in) cotton insertion lace, 4.5–5 cm (1 ¾–2 in) wide
Matching thread
70 cm (27 ½ in) cotton edging lace, 9 cm (3 ½ in) wide
Embroidery thread

1. Draw a line across the width of the fabric 10.5 cm (4 ½ in) away from, and parallel to, the bottom edge of the fabric. Pin the bottom edge of the insertion lace along this line, gently smooth the lace upwards, and pin the top edge of the lace to the fabric. Tack and then machine stitch, using a straight stitch, along both edges of the lace.

2. Working on the wrong side, complete the insertion of the lace (*see* page 38).

3. Make a hem along both long sides of the towel by turning 5 mm (¼ in) and then 1 cm (½ in) to the wrong side; pin, tack and machine stitch, using a straight stitch.

4. Make a hem along the top edge of the towel by turning 5 mm (¼ in) and then 3 cm (1 ¼ in) to the wrong side; pin, tack and machine stitch, using a straight stitch.

5. Make a hem along the bottom edge of the towel by turning 5 mm (¼ in)

3 cm (1 ¼ in) hem along top edge

reverse side of fabric

1 cm (½ in) seam allowance pressed away from bottom edge of lace and tacked

Fig. 89

and then a further 5 cm (2 in) to the wrong side; pin, tack and slip-stitch by hand, enclosing the 1 cm (½ in) seam allowance that was pressed away from the bottom edge of the insertion lace with the top edge of this hem. Neatly slip-stitch the sides of the hem closed.

6. Make a narrow hem along both short ends of the wide edging lace by turning back 5 mm (¼ in) and then 1 cm (½ in). Slip-stitch in place. With right sides together, pin the straight edge of the lace to the lower edge of the hem. Tack and then carefully and neatly slip-stitch the two straight edges together. Press the lace away from the towel.

7. Referring to the instructions for bullion stitch and lazy daisy stitch on pages 15 and 16, and the photograph on page 80, embroider several grub roses and leaves in the centre of the panel of fabric between the insertion lace and the edging lace.

GUEST BATH TOWELS

Plain cotton terry towels can be made to look pretty and feminine with the addition of lace, ribbon, embroidery, and just a little imagination. The instructions given below are general guidelines only; they will provide you with a starting point from which to create your own designs and combinations. Refer to the photograph on page 69, which will give you ideas on how to arrange the lace and ribbon.

Requirements
Cotton insertion and/or edging lace or broderie anglaise
Plain bath or hand towels
Ribbon
Matching thread

1. Carefully wash and iron the cotton lace (*see* page 38).

2. Measure the width of the towel. Each strip of lace or ribbon to be used must be this length, plus an extra 2 cm (¾ in), to allow for hems, and so on. Now cut the lace and ribbon into as many strips of this length as you will require.

3. If you are using edging lace, make a narrow hem at both ends of the lace by turning under 5 mm (¼ in) and then another 5 mm (¼ in). Neatly slip-stitch these hems in place. If you are using insertion lace, turn under 1 cm (½ in) at both ends, and slip-stitch the folded ends to the sides of the towel before machine stitching along the two long sides of the lace using a straight stitch. When stitching ribbon, carefully machine stitch along both long sides of the ribbon using a straight stitch.

RUCHED BLIND

Pure cotton or linen sheets, often left unused in linen cupboards, may be used to make projects that require very little laundering. The ruched blind featured on page 75 was made from a standard double-bed cotton sheet, which adequately covered a window one metre in width.

Calculating the amount of fabric and cotton tape required

WIDTH OF BLIND
Measure the width of the window and double this measurement. Add 5 cm (2 in) for the side hems. If this measurement is greater than the width of the fabric, you will need to make panels and join them. Divide the doubled width measurement by the width of your fabric to determine how many panels you need. If this measurement is not exactly divisible, make one, full centre panel and a narrower panel on either side in order to achieve the desired width.

LENGTH OF BLIND
Measure the height of the window from the curtain rod to the window-sill, and double this measurement. Add a further 11 cm (4 in) for the casing at the top and the hem at the bottom of the blind. (Instead of using tape as a heading, a casing is made at the top, and a wooden rod is pushed through the casing.)

LENGTH OF COTTON TAPE
Measure the length of the blind from the bottom edge of the casing to the base of the blind, without the frill, and multiply this measurement by the number of vertical tapes required: for deep, soft folds use fewer tapes; for more rows of tighter, closely spaced folds, use more tapes. (For example, I used five tapes over a width of 250 cm (100 in), which produced lovely soft, loose folds.)

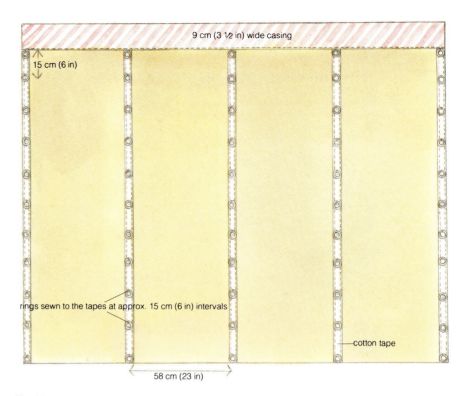

Fig. 90

Requirements
Cotton or linen fabric (or a sheet) of required size (*see* above)
Matching thread
Water-soluble pen
Cotton tape of required length
Cotton edging lace (measuring twice the width of the blind)
Cotton insertion lace (measuring the same as the width of the blind plus 5 cm [2 in])
Plastic curtain rings (enough to sew to the vertical tapes at intervals of about 15 cm [6 in]; *see* Fig. 90)
Wooden rod and 2 brackets
Medium-sized screw-eye
Nylon cord (enough to go up each of the vertical tapes, across the top of the blind and down the side of the blind to the cleat; *see* Fig. 91)
Cleat

Cutting out
1. If a sheet is not used, and the fabric is narrower than the doubled width measurement of the window, cut the fabric into panels and join them with French seams (*see* page 43), so that you have a piece of fabric that

is twice the width and height of the window. Make the hems at the sides of the blind by turning back 5 mm (¼ in) and then another 2 cm (¾ in). Pin, tack and machine stitch, using a straight stitch.

Attaching the tapes
2. Place the fabric, wrong side up, on a flat surface and mark the positions of the vertical tapes with a water-soluble pen. Cut the tape into the required number of lengths, each as long as the blind. Pin a length of tape along each of the side edges of the fabric and the other tapes at equal intervals between them. Tack and machine stitch, using a straight stitch, close to both edges of each length of tape.

Attaching the lace
3. Wash and iron the lace (*see* page 38) and make a narrow hem at both ends of the edging lace by turning back 5 mm (¼ in) and then another 5 mm (¼ in); slip-stitch in place. Gather the edging lace (*see* page 39) and pull up the gathers to fit the

width of the blind. Stitch the straight edge of the edging lace to the bottom of the blind using a French seam (*see* page 43). Iron the seam upwards and tack it to the back of the blind.

4. Turn back 5 mm (¼ in) at both ends of the insertion lace and finger-press. On the right side of the blind, pin the bottom edge of the insertion lace as close as possible to the seam joining the edging lace to the blind, leaving an extra 2 cm (¾ in) of lace at either end. Gently smooth the lace upwards and pin the top edge of the lace to the fabric. At both ends, fold the excess lace towards the back of the blind and pin. Tack and machine stitch through all layers, along both long edges of the lace.

Making the casing

5. Turn back 1 cm (½ in) and then a further 9 cm (3 ½ in) along the top edge of the fabric, and press. Pin, tack and machine stitch close to the edge of this hem.

Attaching the rings

6. Stitch a ring to each of the tapes by hand, just above the frill at the bottom of the blind, making sure that they are in line with one another. Now stitch a ring to each of the tapes just below the casing. Space the rest of the rings evenly, at intervals of approximately 15 cm (6 in).

Hanging the blind

7. Push the wooden rod through the casing, making sure that the casing fits snugly over the rod. Hang the rod on the brackets, and adjust the gathers (on the rod) to fit evenly between the brackets.

8. Screw the screw-eye into the underside of the rod, next to the right-hand edge of the casing (*see* Fig. 91). Cut as many nylon cords as there are vertical tapes (measure out each one individually before cutting, as they will vary in length), and knot one end of each of the cords to one of the

Fig. 91

bottom rings. Thread each cord up through the appropriate vertical line of rings, and then through the top row of rings, towards the screw-eye. Once all the cords have been threaded through the top row of rings and the screw-eye at the side, knot them together, 2–3 cm (¾–1 ¼ in) from the

screw-eye. Cut the cords level with the bottom of the blind, and knot them together again.

9. Screw the cleat to the wall, at the side of the blind and near the bottom of the window. When the blind is pulled up, wind the cords around the cleat in a figure of eight, so that the blind is held in place.

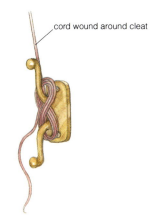

Fig. 92

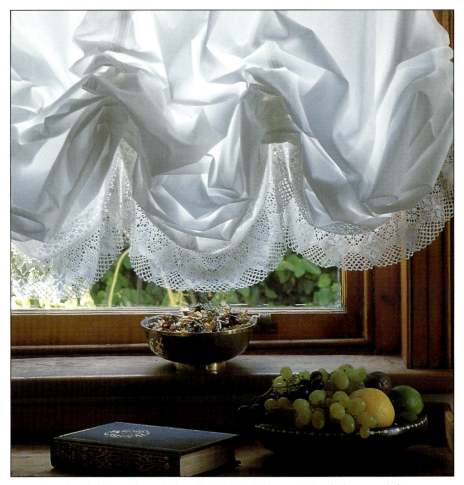

Lovely soft folds are formed when this Ruched Blind (page 74), which was made from a linen sheet, is pulled up.

• FOR THE LIVING-ROOM •

FITTED ROUND TABLECLOTH

This pretty, fitted round tablecloth is especially suitable for a round table with a separate glass top. As there is no standard size for round tables, I have used as an example a table with a diameter of 50 cm (20 in), a circumference of 160 cm (63 ½ in), and a height of 64 cm (25 in).

This method uses a little more fabric than necessary, but the table-cloth looks beautiful and is easier to make. Use the left-over fabric to make another project—a pillowslip, cushion or baby's quilt, for example.

Calculating the amount of fabric required

LENGTH
Measure the circumference of the table top and double this measurement. This is the length of fabric that you will require.

WIDTH
To estimate the width of fabric that you will need, take the following two measurements and add them together:
A: The skirt
Measure from the top edge of the table to the floor. To this measurement, add 2 cm for each tuck. (If you wish to add edging lace to the bottom of the skirt, subtract the width of the edging lace from this total.)
B: The top of the tablecloth
Measure the diameter of the table top, and add on 2 cm (¾ in) to allow for a 1 cm (½ in) seam. You will need a square of fabric with sides of this length—but do not cut it out at this stage. Add this measurement to that for the depth of the skirt. This will be the total width of fabric required.

Calculations for the table used in the example:		
Length of fabric required:		
circumference of table	160 cm	(63 ½ yds)
multiply by two	= 3.2 m	(3 ½ yds)
Width of fabric required:		
A: depth of skirt;	64 cm	(25 in)
add 2 cm (¾ in) for each of four tucks (8 cm)	= 72 cm	(28 in)
subtract width of edging lace	= 62 cm	(24 ½ in)
B: diameter of table top;	50 cm	(20 in)
add 2 cm (¾ in) for seam	= 52 cm	(20 ½ in)
A + B	= 114 cm	(45 in)

To make a fitted round tablecloth to fit the table used in this example, 3.2 m (3 ½ yds) of fabric, 114 cm (45 in) wide, will be required.

If you were purchasing fabric, you would obviously select the nearest width available, which in this case would be 115 cm (45 in).

Requirements
Cotton fabric of required width and length (*see* above)
Brown paper
Matching thread
Cotton insertion lace, the same length as twice the circumference of the table and 5 cm (2 in) wide
Cotton edging lace, the same length as twice the circumference of the table and 10 cm (4 in) wide
Water-soluble pen
Strong yarn

Detail of Fitted Round Tablecloth (this page). The lace curtain in the background creates a soft, dappled light.

Cutting out

1. Referring to Fig. 93 and to Calculating the Amount of Fabric Required, page 77, cut the fabric for the skirt to the correct size. For the table used in this example the length will be 3.2 m (3 ½ yds) and the depth of the skirt will be 62 cm (24 ½ in).

2. Place the brown paper on the table and draw around the edge of the table top. (If the table is not too large, it will be much easier to turn it upside down, place it on top of the paper, and trace around it.) Add on 1 cm (½ in) all around the circumference, to allow for the seam, then cut out the circular shape. This will become the template for the top of the tablecloth. Cut out the tablecloth top from the remaining fabric using the template you have made (*see* Fig. 93).

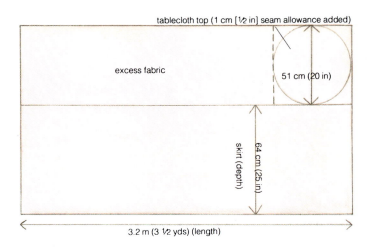

Fig. 93

Attaching lace to skirt

3. Make a neat, narrow hem along the bottom of the skirt by folding back, to the wrong side, 5 mm (¼ in) and then a further 1 cm (½ in). Pin, tack and machine stitch into place using a straight stitch.

4. Wash and iron the insertion and edging lace (*see* page 38). On the right side, pin the straight edge of the edging lace to the edge of the hem, then tack and carefully machine stitch using a straight stitch.

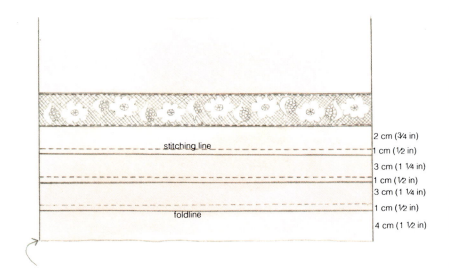

Fig. 94

Making the tucks

5. Referring to Fig. 94, draw three parallel lines along the length of the fabric, the first line 4 cm (1 ½ in) from the straight edge of the lace, the next two, 4 cm (1 ½ in) apart. These will be the foldlines for the tucks. Draw another line 1 cm (½ in) above each of these lines. These will be the stitching lines.

6. Fold the fabric along the foldlines and pin along the stitching lines. Tack and then carefully and neatly machine stitch along the three stitching lines, using a straight stitch.

Inserting the lace

7. Draw another line 2 cm (¾ in) above, and parallel to, the top stitching line. Pin the bottom edge of the insertion lace along this line. Gently smooth the insertion lace upwards and pin the top edge of the insertion lace to the fabric. Tack and then machine stitch, using a straight stitch, along both edges of the lace. Complete the insertion of the lace (*see* page 38).

Completing the side seam

8. Making sure that the two lots of lace and the tucks are properly aligned, complete the side seam, using a French seam (*see* page 43).

Attaching top to skirt

9. Gather the top edge of the fabric for the skirt (*see* Making and Attaching a Fabric Frill, page 42), and pull up the gathers so that the skirt fits the circumference of the outside edge of the tablecloth top. Stay-stitch along the gathering line.

10. With right sides and raw edges together, pin the skirt section to the tablecloth top. Tack and then machine stitch using an overlock stitch or a straight stitch and then a zigzag stitch. Cut away any untidy threads, remove all tacking threads, turn the tablecloth to the right side, and press.

ROUND RUFFLED TABLECLOTH

A pretty tablecloth, draped over a plain round table, will add great charm to an elegant setting, though it will complement almost any décor. Fabric of any width may be used—as long as it covers the tabletop—but instructions are given for fabric of an average width, that is, 115 cm (45 in).

Calculating the amount of fabric required for the frill

Measure the circumference of the cut cloth (see Step 1, below) and double this measurement to calculate the length of the frill strip required. Divide this measurement by the width of the fabric (i.e. 115 cm [45 in]); this will give you the number of strips of fabric you will need to make the frill. Add 2 cm (¾ in) to the length measurement for each strip, to allow for seams.

To calculate the depth of the frill, drape the cut cloth over the table and measure from the edge of the cloth to the floor. Add on 3 cm (1 ¼ in) to allow for a narrow hem along both long sides of the frill. Cut the selvedges off the fabric if they will be noticeable once the tablecloth is complete.

When material is cut on the cross it is inclined to stretch, so it is always advisable to stay-stitch close to the outer edge of a round cloth and also to allow an extra 20 cm (8 in) of fabric when cutting out a frill, if possible, to be on the safe side. There may be a small amount of wastage.

Requirements

115 cm (45 in) fabric,
   115 cm (45 in) wide
String, pencil and pin
Contrasting or matching fabric for frill
   strips, of required width and length
Matching thread
Strong yarn

Cutting out

1. Fold the fabric as shown in Fig. 95. Measure from the top left-hand corner (centre point of fabric) to the top right-hand corner of the folded fabric. Tie the string to the pencil, then cut the string the same length as this measurement. Pin the string as shown in Fig. 95 and, keeping it taut, draw the cutting line with the pencil. Cut the fabric along the cutting line.

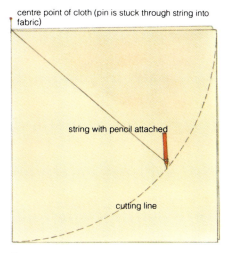

centre point of cloth (pin is stuck through string into fabric)

string with pencil attached

cutting line

Fig. 95   fabric folded into quarters

2. Cut out the number of strips of fabric needed for the frill (see above).

Making and attaching the frill

3. If you are going to use the narrow hemming foot to make the hem along both long sides of the frill, do so on each separate strip of fabric for the frill before completing the seams, as the seams will be too bulky to fit through the metal coil of the narrow hemming foot (see page 9). Join the strips of frill together using French seams (see page 43).

4. Using the strong yarn, gather the frill (see Making and Attaching a Fabric Frill, page 42), making sure that the row of gathering stitches is about 1 cm (½ in) away from the edge of the frill. Pull up the gathers to fit the outside edge of the tablecloth top, and stay-stitch along the gathering line, using a straight stitch. Join the two remaining short sides of the frill using a French seam.

5. Sew a narrow hem around the outside of the cloth, using a narrow hemming foot (see page 9), or a straight and then a zigzag stitch, or overlock the edge (the edge will not be visible once the cloth has been completed).

6. Referring to Fig. 96, and using the gathering line as a guide, pin the wrong side of the frill to the right side of the cloth, close to the edge of the cloth. Tack and machine stitch using a straight stitch. Remove all tacking stitches.

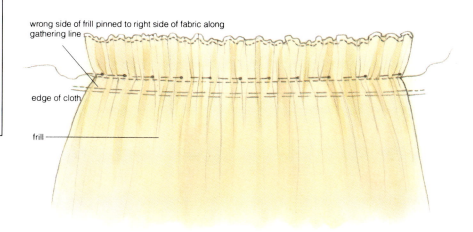

wrong side of frill pinned to right side of fabric along gathering line

edge of cloth

frill

Fig. 96

SMOCKED CUSHION COVER

A piece cut from the outside edge of an old Irish linen sheet was used to make this project. Whatever fabric you use, make sure that it is the same for front and back.

As each person's smocking tension differs slightly, the length of the border and back of the cushion may differ from the measurements given.

Requirements

18 cm x 60 cm (7 in x 24 in) linen, or any other medium-weight fabric
Strong tacking thread
Embroidery thread
1 m (1 ⅛ yds) fabric for the border, 4 cm (1 ½ in) wide
Matching thread
3 m (3 ¼ yds) fabric for the frill, 10 cm (4 in) wide
3 m (3 ¼ yds) cotton edging lace, 2 cm (¾ in) wide
30 cm (12 in) zip
28 cm (11 in) fabric for the back of the cushion, 25 cm (10 in) wide

Smocking

1. Prepare the 18 cm x 60 cm (7 in x 24 in) fabric for smocking by pulling up 22 rows of pleats (*see* page 25). Do not smock the first and last row of pleats. Complete the smocking, referring to Fig. 33, which illustrates the stitch to be used (*see* second variation of Chevron stitch, page 27).

2. Once the smocking and embroidery are complete, set the pleats (*see* page 29) and remove the gathering threads.

Attaching the border

3. Measure the width of the smocked panel and cut the top and bottom strips of border to the same length. With right sides and raw edges together, pin the border to the top edge of the smocked panel. Make sure that the pleats are straight, then tack and machine stitch, using a

straight stitch. Sew the border to the bottom edge of the panel in the same way and press the right side of each border away from the panel.

4. Along the sides, measure the length of the smocked panel plus the two strips of border at the top and bottom, and cut the two side strips of border the same length. With right sides and raw edges together, sew on the side borders, and again press the right side of the borders away from the smocked panel.

Embroidery

5. In each corner, embroider three little roses (*see* Bullion stitch, page 15), each accompanied by three lazy daisy leaves (*see* page 16), as in the photograph below.

Making and attaching the frill

6. Make a narrow hem along one edge of the frill using a narrow hemming foot (*see* page 9), or turn back 5 mm (¼ in) and then 5 mm (¼ in) and

stitch using a straight stitch. On the right side of the fabric, pin the straight edge of the edging lace (with right side uppermost and scallops facing outwards) to the hemmed edge of the frill, and tack and machine stitch using a straight stitch.

7. Gather the frill and pin it, right sides and raw edges together, to the cushion front, leaving 3 cm (1 ¼ in) of gathered frill loose at the ends. Tack and machine stitch the frill to the cushion front (*see* Making and Attaching a Fabric Frill, page 42).

Inserting the zip and completing the cushion cover

8. Insert the zip in the fabric for the back of the cushion cover as described on page 42.

9. Complete the cushion cover by attaching the fabric for the back to the front of the cushion (*see* page 43) and making an inside cushion to fit (*see* page 43).

Detail of Smocked Cushion (this page), showing the positions of the grub roses used in both the embroidery and the smocking.

Smocked Lampshade (this page) showing the position of the smocking, lace and ribbon.

machine stitching, using a straight stitch. Join the strips of frill using French seams (*see* page 43).

5. Wash and iron the lace (*see* page 38). Pin the straight edge of the long strip of lace close to the edge of the hem of the frill, then tack and machine stitch, using a straight stitch.

6. Gather the frill and, with right sides and raw edges together, pin, tack and machine stitch it to the front (*see* Making and Attaching a Fabric Frill, page 42).

Inserting the zip and completing the cushion cover

7. Insert the zip in the fabric for the back of the cover (*see* page 42).

8. Complete the cover by attaching the front to the back, following the instructions on page 43.

9. Make an inside cushion to fit (*see* page 43).

QUILTED CUSHION COVER

Requirements
35 cm x 35 cm (14 in x 14 in) piece of
  cotton or silk fabric for front
35 cm x 35 cm (14 in x 14 in) wadding
35 cm x 35 cm (14 in x 14 in)
  pre-washed muslin
Quilting thread
3.5 m (3 ⅞ yds) cotton or silk, 4 cm
  (1 ½ in) wide, for the frill
Matching thread
3.5 m (3 ⅞ yds) lace,
  4 cm (1 ½ in) wide
40 cm (16 in) zip
35 cm x 37 cm (14 in x 14 ½ in) piece
  of cotton or silk fabric for back

Preparing to quilt
1. Trace the design on page 143 on to the fabric for the front, centring it accurately.

2. Sandwich the wadding between the cushion front and the muslin, then pin and tack the three layers together using either of the methods described on page 33. The more you tack, the easier it will be to quilt.

Quilting
3. Quilt the design using running stitches (*see* page 34). Wash the front when complete, but *do not* iron. Smooth the fabric from the centre to the edges and tack (through all three layers) around the outside edge.

Making and attaching the frill
4. Cut as many strips of cotton or silk for the frill (4 cm [1 ½ in] wide) as are required to make up a 3.5 m (3 ⅞ yds) length when joined. Before joining the strips, make a narrow hem using a narrow hemming foot (*see* page 9), or by turning back 5 mm (¼ in) and then another 5 mm (¼ in) along one side of each strip and pinning, tacking and

SMOCKED LAMPSHADE

These instructions are particularly suitable for an old-fashioned lampshade that is most often used with a 'barley-twist' lampstand.

Calculating the amount of fabric required
Measure the circumference at the base of the lampshade frame (*see* Fig. 98) and add on 2 cm (¾ in) for a seam allowance. This will be the length of the fabric you require. To calculate the width of the fabric to be used, measure from the top metal ring into the 'waist', and from the 'waist' to the bottom metal ring. Add an extra 7 cm (2 ¾ in) to allow for a casing and an overhang at the top, and a hem at the bottom. Now cut out the fabric.

To calculate how much lace is required for each row (there will be two rows), double the measurement of the circumference at the base of the frame.

You will require two lengths of ribbon, each measuring the same as the length of the fabric.

Requirements
Light-weight cotton fabric of required size (*see above*)
Matching thread
Water-soluble pen
Cotton lace of required length
1 large old-fashioned lampshade frame
Strong tacking thread
Satin ribbon, 1 cm (½ in) wide, of required length
Strong yarn or narrow elastic

NOTE *Be sure to buy enough fabric to enable you to make the lampshade using one piece of fabric, so that there will be only one side seam (see Fig. 97). (Any fabric that you may have left over can be used to make another project at a later stage.)*

Making the casing and the hem
1. Make a casing along the top edge of the fabric by turning back 5 mm (¼ in) and then a further 1 cm (½ in) to the wrong side of the fabric. Pin, tack and machine stitch using a straight stitch.

2. Make a narrow hem at the bottom edge of the fabric using a narrow hemming foot (*see* page 9), or by turning 5 mm (¼ in) and then another 5 mm (¼ in) to the wrong side of the fabric. Pin, tack and machine stitch, using a straight stitch. Press the casing and hem flat.

3. Draw a horizontal line 3 cm (1 ¼ in) away from, and parallel to, the bottom hem. Draw another line 10 cm (4 in) away from, and parallel to, the bottom hem. The gathered lace will be stitched to the fabric along these two lines once the smocking is complete.

Smocking
4. To determine where to begin pulling up the pleats for the smocking, measure from the top metal ring to the 'waist' of the frame, and add on 3.5 cm (1 ½ in). (This measurement will probably be about 9 cm [3 ½ in], depending on the size of the frame.) Draw a horizontal line this distance from, and parallel to, the top edge of the casing. This line will become the guideline for pulling up the pleats in preparation for smocking.

5. Pull up six rows of gathering threads (*see* page 25). Do not smock the first and last row; begin smocking on the second row. Complete the smocking and set the pleats (*see* page 29). Remove the gathering theads.

Attaching the lace and the ribbon
6. Wash and iron the lace (*see* page 38) and cut it into two equal lengths. Gather both lengths of lace (*see* page 39) so that each measures the same as the circumference of the base of the frame. Pin the lace to the fabric along the first horizontal line (3 cm [1 ¼ in] from the hem), tack and then stitch it to the fabric (along the gathering line of the lace), using a straight stitch.

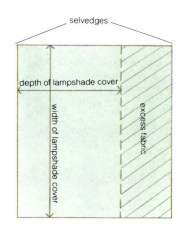

Fig. 97

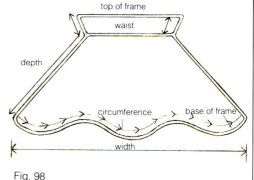

Fig. 98

Fig. 99

7. Pin the ribbon to the fabric so that one edge slightly overlaps the straight edge of the lace, then tack and carefully machine stitch along both long sides of the ribbon.

8. Pin the second piece of lace to the fabric along the second horizontal line (10 cm [4 in] from the hem). Tack and then machine stitch it to the fabric (along the gathering line of the lace) using a straight stitch.

9. Pin, tack and stitch the second length of ribbon to the fabric and the edge of the lace in exactly the same way as you did the first piece of ribbon. Remove the gathering and tacking threads.

10. Stitch the ends of the lace and ribbon to the fabric.

Completing the side seam
11. Carefully aligning the smocking, lace and ribbon, sew the side seam, using a French seam (see page 43).

Fitting the lampshade cover over the frame
12. Place the cover over the frame. The smocking will fit snugly into the 'waist' of the lampshade. Thread the elastic or yarn through the casing and pull it up to fit. Pin the two ends of the elastic together, allowing them to overlap sufficiently, stitch to secure, and cut off the remaining elastic; if using yarn, tie to secure.

13. Being careful to keep the folds of the fabric lying straight, fold the hem over the metal ring at the base of the frame, to the wrong side of the fabric and pin. It may be necessary to ease the fabric along the metal ring as you work. Once the hem has been pinned all the way around the ring, stitch it in place by hand, using small, neat running stitches and matching thread. This part of the project may become a little tedious, but will definitely be well worth the effort, as the finished lampshade is lovely.

ANTIMACASSAR

Antimacassars are washable covers for the back or arm of a chair or sofa. They are so named because they were originally used to protect upholstery from Macassar oil, which was used by men for styling their hair.

Requirements (for one antimacassar)
56 cm x 38 cm (22 in x 15 in) piece of
   linen or other suitable fabric
Matching thread
38 cm (15 in) cotton edging lace,
   10 cm (4 in) wide
1.8 m (2 yds) narrow cotton lace,
   2.5 cm (1 in) wide

Hemming
1. Make a narrow hem along both long sides of the fabric, by turning 5 mm (¼ in) and then another 5 mm (¼ in) to the wrong side of the fabric. Pin, tack and machine stitch using a straight stitch.

2. Make a hem along the top and bottom edges in the same manner.

Attaching the lace
3. Wash and iron both lots of cotton lace (see page 38). Make a narrow hem on both ends of the edging lace as described in Step 1 and, with right side uppermost and scallops facing outwards, pin, tack and stitch the straight edge of this lace to the bottom hem, using a straight stitch.

4. Make a narrow hem at one end of the narrow cotton lace. Beginning at the bottom left-hand corner, pin the lace (right side uppermost and scallops facing outwards) to the two long sides and one short side of the linen, mitring corners (see page 39). At the bottom right-hand corner, make a narrow hem on the short end of the lace. Tack and machine stitch, using a straight stitch (see Fig. 100).

VARIATION
Before hemming any of the edges, sew insertion lace to the front of the fabric, about 6 cm (2 ¼ in) above the straight edge of the wide edging lace. Complete the insertion as described on page 38.

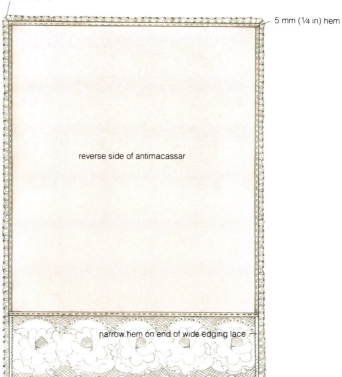

mitred corner of narrow edging lace

5 mm (¼ in) hem

reverse side of antimacassar

narrow hem on end of wide edging lace

narrow hem on short end of lace

Fig. 100

· FOR THE NURSERY ·

As babies have very sensitive skins, choose a soft, pure cotton fabric, such as lawn or a finely woven linen, for making nursery linen. An old, finely woven cotton or linen sheet that is nice and soft will be suitable.

There are usually sections around the outer edges of a sheet (where it has been tucked under the mattress) that are in very good condition, so try to use these. White fabric is practical, as it can be bleached if anything is spilt on the coverlet or pillowslip. It is also advisable to choose a soft cotton lace, especially if the article is to be placed anywhere near the baby's face. Be sure to buy sufficient edging lace to complete the quilt, the pillowslip and the sheet.

QUILTED CRIB COVERLET

Requirements
Tracing paper
Two 54 cm x 42 cm (21 in x 16 ½ in) pieces of fine white fabric
Water-soluble pen
2 m (2 ¼ yds) cotton insertion lace, 5 cm (2 in) wide
Matching thread
4 m (4 ⅜ yds) cotton edging lace, 5 cm (2 in) wide
15 cm (6 in) cotton edging lace, 2 cm (¾ in) wide, for the ruffle around the teddy's neck
52 cm x 40 cm (20 ½ in x 16 in) medium-weight polyester wadding
Quilting thread

Tracing the design
1. Trace the teddy bear and hearts design on page 145 on to tracing paper and then on to one of the 54 cm x 42 cm (21 in x 16 ½ in) pieces of fabric (*see* Tracing the Design on to the Fabric, page 10) in the position

indicated in Fig. 101. Draw a line 9 cm (3 ½ in) from the outside edge, all the way around the fabric using a water-soluble pen.

Completing the front
2. Starting and finishing in the top left-hand corner, and leaving 5 cm (2 in) extra at both ends, pin one edge of the insertion lace along the line you have drawn, carefully mitring all four corners (*see* page 39). Smooth the lace outwards and pin the outer edge of the lace to the fabric. Tack and then machine stitch using a straight stitch, along both edges of the lace.

3. Gather the 5 cm (2 in) wide cotton edging lace and pin it, right sides and raw edges together, to the front of the quilt, leaving 3 cm (1 ¼ in) of gathered lace loose at either end. Tack and then machine stitch the lace to the coverlet front (*see* page 42).

4. Make a very narrow hem (2–3 mm [⅛ in]) at both ends of the 2 cm (¾ in) wide edging lace and gather the lace (*see* page 39). Pull up the gathers to fit the teddy's neck and stitch the gathered lace to the neck by hand, using small running stitches.

Attaching front to back
5. Turn back a 6 mm (¼ in) seam allowance along one short side of each piece of fabric and press. On the front, fold the frill inwards and pin it to the fabric, so that it is not caught in the seam when front and back are stitched together. With right sides and raw edges together, pin and tack the front to the back of the quilt along three sides, leaving the fourth side (on which you turned back the seam allowance) open. Machine stitch, using an overlock stitch, or a straight stitch and then a zigzag stitch. Trim the seam and clip the corners. Turn the coverlet the right way out.

Quilting
6. Slip the wadding inside the coverlet, making sure that you work the corners of the wadding right into the corners of the coverlet. Slip-stitch the opening closed, and prepare the coverlet for quilting by tacking using either of the methods described in Step 3 on page 33. Beginning in the centre of the coverlet, quilt the teddy-bear, and then the hearts (*see* page 34).

Quilt along the inner edge of the insertion lace, and then, if you wish, quilt along one of the designs in the centre of the lace. Lastly, quilt along the outer edge of the insertion lace, and remove all the tacking threads. The coverlet may be washed but not ironed.

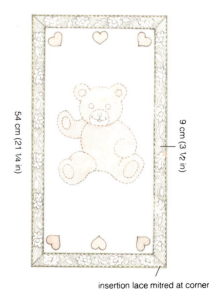

42 cm (16 ½ in)

54 cm (21 ¼ in)

9 cm (3 ½ in)

insertion lace mitred at corner

Fig. 101

CRIB OR PRAM PILLOWSLIP

Requirements

31 cm (12 in) fabric to match the
sheet, 115 cm (45 in) wide
1.4 m (1 ½ yds) cotton insertion lace,
2.5 cm (1 in) wide
3 m (3 ¼ yds) cotton edging lace,
5 cm (2 in) wide
Water-soluble pen
Matching thread
Embroidery thread

Cutting out

1. Cut the fabric into one 38 cm x
31 cm (15 in x 12 in) piece for the
front, one 39 cm x 31 cm (15 ¼ in x
12 in) piece for the back, and one
31 cm x 12 cm (12 in x 4 ¾ in) piece
for the flap.

2. Wash and iron the lace (*see* page
38) and cut the insertion lace into two
pieces measuring 38 cm (15 in) each,
and two measuring 31 cm (12 in) each.

3. Place the fabric for the front of the
pillowslip on a flat surface and draw a
line 5 cm (2 in) away from, and
parallel to, each of the four sides.
These will be lines A, B, C and D.

*Detail of Crib or Pram Pillowslip (*this page*) and Crib Sheet (*page 87*).*

Attaching the lace

4. Pin one edge of one of the 38 cm
(15 in) lengths of insertion lace along
line A. Gently smooth the lace
outwards and pin the other edge of
the lace to the fabric. Tack and then
machine stitch, along both edges of
the lace, using a straight stitch. Stitch
the other 38 cm (15 in) length of
insertion lace to line B and the two
31 cm (12 in) lengths of insertion lace
to lines C and D in the same manner
as the first. Stitch the ends of the lace
to the fabric close to the raw edges of
the fabric, to ensure that they will be
caught in the seams.

5. Gather the edging lace (*see* page
39). Stitch the gathered lace to the
front of the pillowslip (*see* Making and
Attaching a Fabric Frill, page 42).

Completing the pillowslip

6. Work the embroidered roses (*see*
Bullion stitch, page 15) in the
positions indicated in Fig 102.

7. Complete the pillowslip, following
Steps 13–16 on page 48, the only
difference being that in Step 14, 5 mm
(¼ in) and then a further 5 mm (¼ in)
is turned back along one short side of
the fabric for the back of the
pillowslip. Remove all tacking threads.

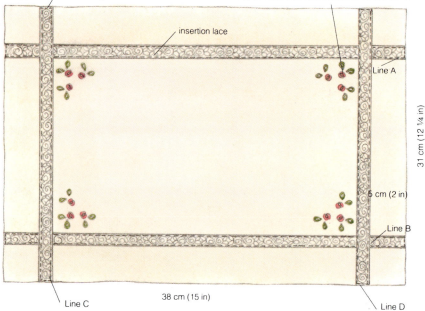

end of lace stitched to raw edge of fabric

three grub roses each accompanied by two leaves

insertion lace

Line A

Line B

Line C

Line D

31 cm (12 ¼ in)

5 cm (2 in)

38 cm (15 in)

Fig. 102

CRIB SHEET

This pretty crib sheet can easily be adapted to fit a doll's crib, as can the Crib or Pram Pillowslip (page 86) and Quilted Crib Coverlet (page 85).

Requirements

80 cm (31 ½ in) insertion lace, 2 cm (¾ in) wide (same as pillowslip)
1 m x 80 cm (1 ⅛ yds x 31 ½ in) fabric for the sheet
Matching thread
80 cm (31 ½ in) edging lace, 5 cm (2 in) wide (to match that used for the pillowslip)
79 cm (31 ½ in) satin ribbon, 1 cm (½ in) wide (to match that used for the pillowslip)
Embroidery thread

Inserting the lace

1. Wash and iron the lace following the instructions on page 38.

2. Place the fabric on a flat surface (with right side uppermost) and draw a line 6.5 cm (2 ½ in) from, and parallel to, one of the short sides of the fabric. Pin one edge of the insertion lace along this line, then gently smooth the lace upwards and pin the top edge of the lace to the fabric. Tack and machine stitch along both edges of the lace, using a straight stitch.

3. Working on the wrong side of the fabric, carefully cut along the centre of the fabric behind the insertion lace. Complete the top hem of the insertion lace following the instructions given on page 38, and press the 1 cm (½ in) seam allowance along the bottom edge of the insertion lace away from the lace.

Hemming

4. Make a narrow hem along the other three sides of the sheet by turning back 5 mm (¼ in) and then a further 5 mm (¼ in). Pin, tack and machine stitch using a straight stitch.

5. Turn back 5 mm (¼ in) and then a further 3 cm (1 ½ in) along the remaining edge of the sheet so that the top edge of the hem meets the bottom edge of the insertion lace (the 1 cm [½ in] turned-back flap is enclosed in this hem); pin, tack and slip-stitch by hand. Press the hem.

Attaching the edging lace and ribbon

6. Make a narrow hem at both ends of the edging lace by turning back 5 mm (¼ in) and then another 5 mm (¼ in); slip-stitch in place. Pin the straight edge of the edging lace to the edge of the sheet as shown in Fig. 103a). Tack and machine stitch into place using a straight stitch.

7. Turn back 5 mm (¼ in) on both ends of the ribbon; pin one edge of the ribbon to the sheet, slightly overlapping the straight edge of the edging lace. Tack and machine stitch along both edges of the ribbon and embroider three roses and four leaves in the centre of the ribbon (*see* Bullion stitch, page 15 and Lazy daisy stitch, page 16). Remove tacking threads.

80 cm (31 ½ in)

1 m (1 ⅛ yds)

narrow hem stitched around three sides of sheet

2 cm (¾ in) wide insertion lace

straight edge of edging lace pinned to edge of sheet

Fig. 103a

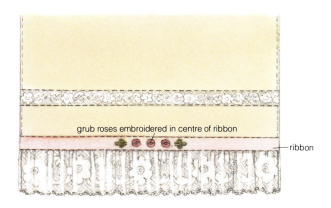

grub roses embroidered in centre of ribbon

ribbon

Fig. 103b

CRIB SKIRT AND PETTICOAT

Decorate a wicker crib with a pretty skirt and petticoat using these easy instructions. Select a fabric that is easy to launder so that the skirt may be kept clean without too much trouble. Suitable fabrics include cotton lawn, broderie anglaise, closely woven lace (so that the baby's fingers will not become entangled), or any other fine cotton fabric.

Requirements
Wicker crib (without a hood)
    on a stand
Brown paper or newspaper to make a
    template
3.8 m x 97 cm (4 ¼ yds x 38 in) fine
    cotton fabric for the skirt
Matching thread
3.8 m (4 ¼ yds) cotton lace or
    broderie anglaise, 9 cm (3 ½ in)
    wide, for the skirt
3.8 m (4 ¼ yds) satin ribbon, at least
    1 cm (½ in) wide
Water-soluble pen
3.8 m (4 ¼ yds) cotton tape, 2 cm
    (¾ in) wide, for the casing
1.9 m (2 yds) narrow elastic,
    for the skirt
3.8 m x 66 cm (4 ¼ yds x 26 in) cotton
    fabric or net, for the petticoat
3.8 m (4 ¼ yds) cotton lace or
    broderie anglaise, 9 cm (3 ½ in)
    wide, for the petticoat
1.9 m (2 yds) narrow elastic
    for the petticoat
Net for the base of the skirt

Cutting out
1. Pin the template of the base of the crib to the net, trace around the template, and cut out.

The skirt
2. Make a narrow hem along the bottom edge of the fabric for the skirt by turning back 5 mm (¼ in) and then a further 5 mm (¼ in). Pin, tack and machine stitch.

Calculating the amount of fabric required for the skirt
Press the paper (see Requirements, below) flat onto the base of the inside of the crib. Make a crease around the circumference of the base with your fingernail and draw around the crease with a pencil. Remove the paper, add 1 cm (½ in) all around the circumference for a seam allowance, and cut out the template. Take the following measurements:
A: Measure the circumference of the template and double the measurement.

B: The fabric for the inner lining and the outer skirt of the crib are cut in one piece. On the inside, measure from the base to the rim, over the rim (towards the outside of the crib) to about 5 cm (2 in) below the rim, where the casing for the elastic is to be placed.

C: Continue to measure until you reach about 15 cm (6 in) above the floor; then add a further 2 cm (¾ in) to this measurement for seam allowances. For example, for the crib photographed on page 84 the measurements were as follows:

A: 190 cm (75 in) x 2
    = 3.8 m (4 ¼ yds)
B: 38 cm (15 in)
C: 97 cm (38 in)

Calculating the amount of fabric required for the petticoat
On the outside of the crib, measure from just beneath the outer edge of the top rim to about 9 cm (3 ½ in) above the floor; add 3 cm (1 ¼ in) to this measurement to allow for a casing and a hem. For the crib used as an example, this measurement was 66 cm (26 in).

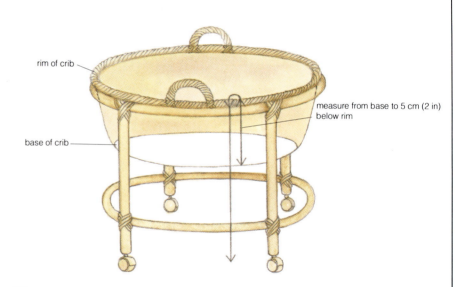

rim of crib

base of crib

measure from base to 5 cm (2 in) below rim

Fig. 104

3. If you are going to use cotton lace for the edge of the skirt, wash the lace following the instructions on page 38. (Broderie anglaise does not require the same treatment, as it is pre-shrunk.) Pin the straight edge of the lace or broderie anglaise to the edge of the hem; tack and machine stitch using a straight stitch. Pin the satin ribbon along the straight edge of the cotton lace or broderie anglaise, making sure that one long edge of the ribbon slightly overlaps the edge of the lace. Tack and machine stitch along both edges of the ribbon.

4. On the wrong side of the fabric, draw a horizontal line, parallel to the top edge of the fabric, using measurement B (see above). To make the casing, pin one long edge of the cotton tape to this line, smooth the tape upwards, and pin the other edge to the fabric. Tack and machine stitch close to both edges of the tape.

5. Thread one length of the elastic through the casing, first making sure that the loose end of the elastic is properly secured. Then stitch both ends of the elastic to the sides of the fabric by hand.

6. Sew the two short ends of the skirt together using a French seam (*see* page 43), making sure that the lace or broderie anglaise and the satin ribbon are correctly aligned.

7. Gather the top edge of the skirt (*see* Making and Attaching a Fabric Frill, page 42) and pull the gathers up to fit the net that forms the base of the skirt. With right sides together, pin the gathered edge of the skirt to the edge of the net. Tack and machine stitch using an overlock stitch or a straight and then a zigzag stitch. Trim any ragged threads and remove all tacking threads. Turn the skirt the right way out.

The petticoat
8. Make a hem along the bottom edge of the fabric for the petticoat by turning back 5 mm (¼ in) and then a further 5 mm (¼ in). Pin, tack and machine stitch using a straight stitch.

9. Pin the straight edge of the second length of lace to the edge of the hem, then tack and machine stitch using a straight stitch.

10. Sew the two short sides of the petticoat together using a French seam (*see* page 43).

11. Make a casing at the top edge of the petticoat by turning back 5 mm (¼ in) and then a further 1 cm (½ in). Pin, tack and machine stitch close to the edge of the hem of the casing leaving a small opening through which the elastic may be threaded.

12. Thread the elastic through the casing and pin the ends together. Place the petticoat over the crib sides and pull the elastic tight enough to

prevent the petticoat from slipping off the crib. Remove the petticoat, stitch the ends of the elastic together securely and neatly stitch the opening closed by hand. Turn the right way out and remove all tacking threads.

Fitting the skirt and petticoat
13. Position the petticoat so that the top of the casing is just below the outer edge of the top rim. Place the net base of the skirt on the bottom of the crib. Place the mattress on top of the net and pull the skirt over the top rim of the crib, making sure that the casing lies just below the outer edge of the rim. Adjust the gathers so that they are evenly spaced.

LACE-EDGED NET CRIB COVER

If, like me, you kept your wedding veil for sentimental reasons, you can put it to good use now by turning it into a net crib cover for keeping insects away from your baby while he or she is sleeping.

Net or chiffon, which can be purchased from most haberdashery shops, may be substituted very successfully if you do not have a veil.

This net crib cover may be used as a tea-shower at a later stage.

Requirements
1.2 m (1 ¼ yds) net,
   1.5 cm (¾ in) wide
5.6 m (6 ¼ yds) cotton edging lace,
   7 cm (2 ¾ in) wide
Matching thread
6.04 m (6 ½ yds) satin ribbon, 1 cm
   (½ in) wide
Embroidery thread

Hemming
1. Make a narrow hem along all four sides of the net by turning back 5 mm (¼ in) and then a further 5 mm (¼ in) to the wrong side. Pin, tack and machine stitch using a straight stitch.

Attaching the lace and ribbon
2. Wash and iron the cotton edging lace (*see* page 38). Lay the net on a flat surface and, beginning and ending in the top right-hand corner and leaving an extra 8 cm (3 in) at both ends, pin the lace (right side uppermost) to the edge of the hem along all four sides, carefully mitring the corners (*see* page 39). When you reach the top right-hand corner, carefully mitre the fourth corner. Tack and machine stitch using a straight stitch.

3. Leaving 15 cm (6 in) loose at either end of each of the four satin ribbons, pin the ribbons along the inside edges of the lace, as shown in Fig. 105. Make sure that one edge of each ribbon slightly overlaps the edge of the lace. Using a straight stitch, tack and machine stitch along both edges of each of the lengths of ribbon, stopping about 1 cm (½ in) away from each of the corners. Tie bows at each corner of the cover. Embroider grub roses (*see* Bullion stitch, page 15) and leaves (*see* Lazy daisy stitch, page 16) in the positions shown in Fig. 105, or stitch lace motifs cut from scraps of lace in each corner. Remove all tacking threads.

Fig. 105

DOLL'S CRIB QUILT

Porcelain dolls have become very popular again, and look most attractive if displayed in an old doll's crib or pram. Even more important, children love to play with beautiful toys, and if this set of dolls' linen is made from fabric that is easy to launder, it will give them many hours of pleasure without creating extra work. This is also another way of using up fairly small pieces of linen or lawn sheeting, and short lengths of cotton lace or broderie anglaise.

Alternatively, if you are short of time but wish to make these projects, use an embroidered place-mat or tray-cloth. Beautiful tray-cloths that have been hand-embroidered in the East, are inexpensive and readily available, as are old tray-cloths, which can be found in second-hand or antique shops. The doll's crib quilt featured on this page was made from a tray-cloth.

Requirements
3 m (3 ¼ yds) cotton edging lace or broderie anglaise, of desired width
46 cm x 32 cm (18 ½ in x 12 ½ in) tray-cloth
Matching thread
46 cm x 32 cm (18 ½ in x 12 ½ in) similar white fabric
45 cm x 31 cm (18 in x 12 in) medium-weight wadding
Quilting thread

NOTE *The seam allowance for this project is 5 mm (¼ in).*

Attaching the lace
1. Wash and iron the cotton edging lace (*see* page 38).

2. Gather the lace (*see* page 39) and, with right sides and raw edges together, pin it to the front of the tray-cloth, leaving 3 cm (1 ¼ in) of gathered lace loose at either end.

A beautiful antique crib provides the perfect background for the Doll's Crib Quilt (this page).

Tack and then machine stitch the lace to the quilt front (*see* Making and Attaching a Fabric Frill, page 42). Fold the lace frill inwards, and pin it to the fabric, so that it does not become caught in the seam.

Attaching front to back
3. Turn back a 5 mm (¼ in) seam allowance along one short edge of the front and the back of the quilt, and press. With right sides and raw edges together, pin and tack the front to the back of the quilt along three sides, leaving the fourth side open (this will be the side on which you have turned

back the seam allowances). Machine stitch, using an overlock stitch, or a straight stitch and then a zigzag stitch. Trim away all ragged threads and clip the corners. Turn the quilt the right way out.

4. Slip the wadding inside the quilt, working the corners of the wadding right into the corners of the quilt. Slip-stitch the opening closed, and prepare the quilt for quilting as described on page 32. Quilt those parts of the design that you wish to accentuate (*see* page 34). Remove the tacking threads.

DOLL'S CRIB PILLOWSLIP

Choose similar fabric to that used for the quilt; a finer fabric can also be used. Make the inside cushion (*see* page 43) using fabric of a pale colour, which will show through the insertion lace and look very pretty.

Requirements

20 cm x 26 cm (8 in x 10 in) fabric for the front
Water-soluble pen
2 m (2 ¼ yds) edging lace, 5 cm (2 in) wide
42 cm (16 ½ in) insertion lace, 2 cm (¾ in) wide
65 cm (25 ½ in) edging lace, 3 cm (1 ¼ in) wide
Matching thread
42 cm (16 ½ in) satin ribbon, 1 cm (½ in) wide
20 cm x 27 cm (8 in x 10 ½ in) fabric for the back
20 cm x 7 cm (8 in x 2 ¾ in) fabric for the flap

Attaching the lace

1. Place the 20 cm x 26 cm (8 in x 10 in) piece of fabric on a flat surface and draw a line parallel to, and 5 cm (¼ in) away from, the right-hand edge.

2. Wash and iron the lace (*see* page 38) and cut the insertion lace into two equal lengths. Pin one edge of one length of insertion lace along this line. Gently smooth the insertion lace to the left and pin the other edge to the fabric. Tack and machine stitch along both edges of the lace using a straight stitch. Complete the insertion of the lace (*see* page 38).

3. Cut the 3 cm (1 ¼ in) wide edging lace into two equal lengths and gather both lengths (*see* page 39). Working with one length of the lace, carefully pull up the gathers until it measures 21 cm (8 ¼ in), and pin the straight edge of the edging lace next to the edge of the insertion lace (*see* Fig. 106a). Tack and then machine stitch using a zigzag stitch, so that the gathers along the straight edge of the lace are flattened.

Detail of Doll's Crib Pillowslip (this page) and Doll's Crib Quilt (page 90) showing the insertion and edging lace, and the satin ribbon.

4. Cut the ribbon into two equal lengths and pin one edge of one length so that it slightly overlaps the outside edge of the insertion lace. Pin the other edge of the ribbon through the edging lace to the fabric beneath (*see* Fig. 106b). Tack and then machine stitch along both edges of the ribbon, using a straight stitch.

5. Turn the fabric around and complete the second half of the front of the pillowslip in exactly the same manner. Tack the loose ends of the edging lace to the fabric.

6. Gather the 5 cm (2 in) wide edging lace (*see* page 39) and pin the gathered lace, right sides and raw edges together, to the front of the pillowslip and stitch (*see* Making and Attaching a Fabric Frill, page 42).

Completing the pillowslip

7. Complete the pillowslip, following Steps 13–16 on page 48, the only difference being that in Step 13, 5 mm (¼ in) and then another 5 mm (¼ in) is turned back along one short side of the fabric for the back of the pillowslip. Remove all tacking threads and turn the right way out.

Fig. 106a

straight edge of edging lace next to edge of insertion lace

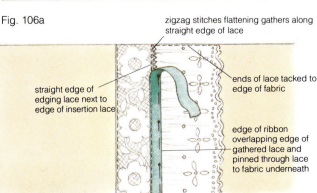

Fig. 106b

zigzag stitches flattening gathers along straight edge of lace

straight edge of edging lace next to edge of insertion lace

ends of lace tacked to edge of fabric

edge of ribbon overlapping edge of gathered lace and pinned through lace to fabric underneath

CLOTHING FOR BABIES AND CHILDREN

CHRISTENING ROBE

This christening robe will fit babies of average size, from a few weeks to about six months of age.

Requirements

1.3 m (1 ½ yds) fine white cotton lawn, 115 cm (45 in) wide
Tracing paper
Water-soluble pen
Matching thread
30 cm (12 in) cotton insertion lace, 1.5 cm (⅝ in) wide, for front yoke
1 m (1 ⅛ yds) cotton edging lace, 1.5 cm (⅝ in) wide
27 cm (10 ¾ in) bias strip, 2 cm (¾ in) wide, cut from the same fabric as robe
5.4 m (6 yds) broderie anglaise insertion, 3.5 cm (1 ½ in) wide
3.6 m (4 yds) fine cotton insertion lace, 5 cm (2 in) wide
3.6 m (4 yds) broderie anglaise edging, 14–15 cm (5 ½–6 in) wide
Two 30 cm (12 in) bias strips, 2 cm (¾ in) wide, cut from the same fabric as robe
Narrow elastic
3 little pearl buttons

Cutting out

1. Cut out two pieces of lawn, each measuring 65 cm x 90 cm (25 ½ in x 35 ½ in), for the front and back of the skirt section.

2. Trace the patterns on pages 147–149 for the back and front yokes and sleeve and cut them out.

3. Place the front yoke pattern on the fabric and trace around it. Do the same for the two halves of the back yoke and the sleeves. Cut out the sleeves. Remove the pattern pieces from the bodice sections. Before cutting out, stay-stitch around the outside edges to prevent the fabric from fraying. Cut out the two halves of the back yoke.

Inserting the lace

4. Do *not* cut out the front yoke yet. Mark on the front yoke where the strips of insertion lace are to be placed. After washing and ironing the lace (*see* page 38) cut the strips of insertion lace slightly longer than required. Pin these strips to the front yoke, then tack and carefully machine stitch, using a straight stitch, along both edges of each strip of lace. Now cut out the front yoke.

5. Working on the wrong side, carefully cut away the fabric behind each strip of lace, leaving 6 mm (¼ in) of fabric inside each line of stitching. Make tiny neat hems by turning back 3 mm (⅛ in) and then another 3 mm (⅛ in). Finger-press, tack and stitch each hem neatly in place by hand.

Hemming the back yokes

6. On the centre back edge of both halves of the back yoke, turn back 5 mm (¼ in) and then another 1 cm (½ in) to the wrong side. Pin, tack and neatly slip-stitch the hems in place by hand.

Shoulder seams

7. Stitch the front yoke to the two halves of the back yoke at the shoulders, using French seams (*see* page 43).

Neck edge

8. Cut the cotton edging lace into three strips, one measuring 40 cm (16 in) and two measuring 30 cm (12 in) each. On the bias strip measuring 27 cm x 2 cm (10 ½ in x ¾ in) turn back 5 mm (¼ in) at both ends and along one long side, and finger-press. With right sides together, pin the other long side of the bias strip to the neck edge. Tack and then machine stitch using a straight stitch. Now stitch the neck edge a second time, just inside the first stitching line, to strengthen it. Trim the seam and fold the binding towards the wrong side of the neck edge. Pin, tack and slip-stitch in place.

9. Make a narrow hem at each end of the 40 cm (16 in) strip of edging lace by turning under 3 mm (⅛ in) and then 3 mm (⅛ in); slip-stitch. Carefully gather the lace (*see* page 39), very close to the straight edge, so that it measures 25 cm (10 in). With right sides together, pin the straight edge of the lace to the neck edge; slip-stitch the straight edge of the lace to the top edge of the binding.

Skirt front

10. With a water-soluble pen, draw three parallel lines horizontally across the fabric (these will be the foldlines for the tucks), the first being 3.5 cm (1 ½ in) from the bottom of the fabric and the next two, 2.5 cm (1 in) apart (*see* Fig. 107b). Make a fold along the first of the parallel lines. Place the edge of the sewing foot on the edge of the fold, and stitch, using a straight stitch. Stitch the other two tucks in the same way. Place a damp cloth over the tucks and press, so that the tucks all face downwards. Make a narrow hem along the bottom of the fabric, using a narrow hemming foot (*see* page 9), or by turning under 5 mm (¼ in) and then another 5 mm (¼ in); pin, tack and machine stitch, using a straight stitch.

11. Cut the 5.4 m (6 yds) broderie anglaise insertion into six strips, each measuring 90 cm (35 ½ in). Set three strips aside for the skirt back. Cut the 3.6 m (4 yds) cotton insertion lace into four strips, each measuring 90 cm (35 ½ in) and set two aside for the back. Cut the wide broderie anglaise edging into two strips, each measuring 1.8 m (2 yds). Set one strip aside for the skirt back.

12. To complete the lower lacy section of the skirt, study Fig. 107c carefully, then pin three strips of broderie anglaise insertion and two strips of cotton insertion lace together (one by one, and with right sides together, along their long edges), in the following order: the first, third and fifth strips are broderie anglaise, and the second and fourth are cotton insertion lace. Tack and then carefully slip-stitch the strips together, so that only the edges meet.

13. Overlock or use a straight and then a zigzag stitch along the top edge of the wide broderie anglaise edging, turn back 5 mm (¼ in) to the wrong side, and press flat. Gather very close to the folded edge (*see* page 39) and pull up the gathers so that the edging measures 90 cm (35 ½ in). With right sides together, pin the top edge of the broderie anglaise edging to the lower edge of the last strip of insertion, then tack and carefully slip-stitch the two edges together.

14. Now that the lacy section is complete, sew it to the lower edge of the skirt front: with right sides together, pin the top edge of the first strip of insertion to the lower edge of the skirt front, then tack and slip-stitch the two edges together.

15. Gather the upper edge of the skirt front and pull up the gathers to fit the lower edge of the front yoke (*see* page 42). Machine stitch the skirt front to the front yoke using a French seam (*see* page 43).

Skirt back

16. Complete the skirt back in the same way as the skirt front, as described in Steps 10, 12, 13 and 14.

17. Make a placket in the skirt back (*see* page 42), and gather the top edge of both sections of the skirt back (*see* page 42). Pull up the gathers to fit the bottom edge of the back yokes. Sew the two sections of the skirt back to the two back yokes, using French seams (*see* page 43).

Sleeves

18. Along the lower edge of the sleeves, turn 5 mm (¼ in) and then a further 5 mm (¼ in) to the wrong side. Pin, tack and then machine stitch, using a straight stitch. With right side uppermost, pin the straight edge of each of the short strips of narrow edging lace to the lower edge of both sleeves (on the right side), then tack and machine stitch carefully, using a straight stitch.

19. Turn in 5 mm (¼ in) on both long edges of each of the 30 cm x 2 cm (12 in x ¾ in) bias strips, and press. To make the casing for the elastic, pin the bias strip, with folds down, to the wrong side of the sleeves, in the position marked on the sleeve pattern. Tack and stitch close to both edges of the casings.

20. To gather the top of the sleeves, stitch along the seam line and again just inside the seam line, between the small dots, using very long machine stitches. *Do not* pull up the gathers at this stage.

Setting sleeves into armholes

21. With right sides together, pin the sleeve to the armhole edge, matching small dots. Pull up the gathers at the top of the sleeve to fit the armhole. Pin, tack and machine stitch using an overlock stitch, or a straight stitch and then a zigzag stitch. Trim the seam. Repeat for second sleeve. Cut two pieces of elastic, each the baby's

wrist measurement plus an extra 3 cm (1 ¼ in). Thread the elastic through the casings and secure by hand stitching the ends of the elastic to the fabric.

Side seams

22. Make quite sure that the tucks, broderie anglaise insertion, cotton insertion lace and broderie anglaise edging are properly aligned, and stitch the entire side seam (from the edge of the sleeve to the lower edge of the skirt) in one continuous seam, using a French seam (*see* page 43). Stitch the second side seam in the same way. Remove all tacking threads.

Completing the robe

23. Sew three little pearl buttons to the right-hand back yoke, spacing them evenly. On the left-hand back yoke, make three loops large enough for a button to pass through, using buttonhole stitch (*see* page 43), to correspond with the three buttons.

Fig. 107a

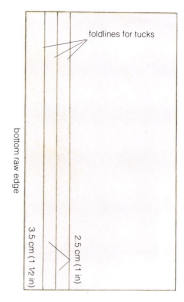

Fig. 107b

Fig. 107c

broderie anglaise edging

edges slip-stitched together

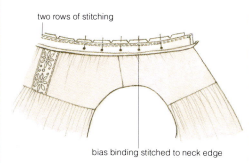

two rows of stitching

bias binding stitched to neck edge

Fig. 107d

Attaching the edging

2. Gather the broderie anglaise edging (*see* page 39) until it measures 164 cm (64 ½ in). Pin, tack and then machine stitch the gathered edge of the broderie anglaise edging to the skirt using a narrow French seam (*see* page 43).

Side seams

3. Stitch the short sides of the fabric together using a French seam, but leave an 18 cm (7 in) opening (*see* Fig. 108a). Bind the opening (*see* Making a Placket, page 42) and then press the seam flat.

Making the tucks

4. Sew the tucks as follows: make a fold along the first of the parallel lines. Place the edge of the sewing foot on the edge of the fold and stitch, using a straight stitch. Sew the other four tucks in the same manner. Place a damp cloth over the tucks and press, so that they all face downwards.

Gathering the skirt and attaching the waistband

5. Gather the top edge of the fabric (*see* Making and Attaching a Fabric Frill, page 42) until it measures 45 cm (18 in). With right sides together, pin and tack the waistband to the waist edge of the skirt, matching large dots. (The seam allowance for the waist edge of the skirt and all seams on the waistband is 1 cm [½ in]). Machine stitch, using a straight stitch. Trim the seam allowance.

6. With right sides together, fold the waistband along the foldline, stitch the ends as shown, clipping back to the large dot. Trim the seam allowances at both ends, and trim across the corners. Turn back 1 cm (½ in) along the remaining seam line, and press. Turn the waistband the right way out and press. Hem the waistband to the wrong side of the skirt, using small, neat stitches. Sew the press-studs in place.

CHRISTENING PETTICOAT

Requirements

Water-soluble pen
84 cm x 164 cm (33 in x 64 ½ in) fine
    white lawn (or other white cotton)
Matching thread
3.5 m (3 ⅞ yds) broderie anglaise
    edging, 14–15 cm (5 ½–6 in) wide
    (it is preferable to use the same
    edging as for the christening robe)
10 cm x 54 cm (4 in x 21 in) strip of
    matching fabric, for the waistband
2 press-studs

I. With a water-soluble pen, draw five horizontal lines 2.5 cm (1 in) apart and parallel to the edge, across the width of the fabric (*see* Fig. 108a).

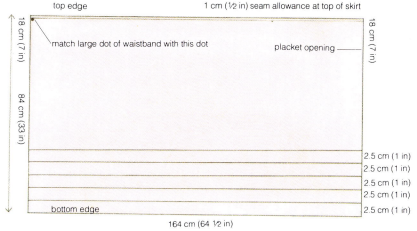

top edge

18 cm (7 in)

match large dot of waistband with this dot

1 cm (½ in) seam allowance at top of skirt

placket opening

18 cm (7 in)

84 cm (33 in)

2.5 cm (1 in)
2.5 cm (1 in)
2.5 cm (1 in)
2.5 cm (1 in)
2.5 cm (1 in)

bottom edge

164 cm (64 ½ in)

Fig. 108a

sew to gathered fabric

foldline

1 cm (½ in) seam allowance

clip back to large dot

Fig. 108b

CHRISTENING BIB

Requirements
Tracing paper
Water-soluble pen
2 pieces of white lawn, each 16 cm x
   21 cm (6 ¼ in x 8 ¼ in)
16 cm x 21 cm (6 ¼ in x 8 ¼ in) thin
   white wadding
Matching thread
Strong tacking thread
Quilting thread
22.5 cm (9 in) bias strip, 1.5 cm (⅝ in)
   wide, cut from the white lawn
1.06 m (1 ¼ yds) cotton lace, 1.5 cm
   (⅝ in) wide
1 small mother-of-pearl button

Cutting out
1. Trace off the pattern and the design
on page 151. Trace the outline and
design on to one of the pieces of
lawn. Pin the two pieces of fabric
together and cut the bib shape out
along the outline. Cut out a piece of
wadding using the same pattern.

Attaching front to back
2. With right sides together, pin, tack
and stitch the two pieces of the bib
together around the outer edges,
using an overlock stitch or a straight
stitch and then a zigzag stitch. Do not
stitch along the neck edge. Carefully
turn the right way out, and press.

3. Slip the wadding between the two
pieces of fabric, carefully easing it so
that it fits correctly. Tack around the
outer edge, including the neck edge.

Quilting
4. Tack the whole bib using radiating
lines of stitches (*see* page 33); quilt (*see*
English Quilting, page 34).

Neck edge
5. Baste the neck edge very close to
the edge of the fabric. On one end of
the bias strip, turn back 5 mm (¼ in)
towards the wrong side. With right
sides together, pin the bias binding
along the stitching line of the neck

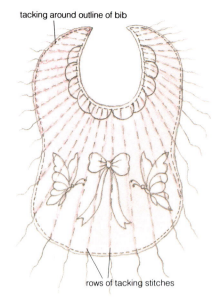

tacking around outline of bib

rows of tacking stitches

Fig. 109

edge. Turn back 5 mm (¼ in) on the
other end of the bias strip. Tack and
then stitch along the stitching line.
(When stitching around the curve of
the neck, gently pull the edge into a
straight line.) Sew a second row of
stitches inside the first row of
stitches. Clip the curves and trim
away any ragged threads or fabric.
Turn back 5 mm (¼ in) along the
remaining long side of the bias strip
and fold it over to the back of the bib.
Pin, tack and hand stitch the binding
into place, using tiny, neat hemming
stitches. Slip-stitch both ends of the
bias strip closed.

Attaching the lace
6. Gather the lace (*see* page 39) and
make a narrow hem by turning back
5 mm (¼ in) and then a further 5 mm
(¼ in) at each end of the lace. With
right sides together, and starting at
the top left-hand corner of the neck
edge, pin the straight edge of the lace
to the outside edge of the bib, very
close to the edge. Tack and then hand
stitch the lace to the bib using tiny,
neat running stitches and making
sure that the stitches go right through
all three layers. This will quilt the
edge and keep the wadding in place.

Finishing off
7. Sew the little button to the top
right-hand tip of the bib. Embroider a
little loop on the top left-hand tip of
the bib using buttonhole stitch (*see*
page 43), ensuring that the loop is
large enough for the button to pass
through.

8. Remove all tacking threads and
wash the bib to remove the marking
pen ink. *Do not* iron.

CHILD'S SMOCKED DRESS

This dress will fit a child of
two-and-a-half to three years of age,
the finished length being about 49 cm
(19 ½ in) and the chest measurement
being approximately 56 cm (22 in).

Requirements
Tracing paper
Water-soluble pen
1.75 m (1 ¾ yds) cotton fabric,
   115 cm (45 in) wide
Strong tacking thread
Embroidery thread
Matching thread
1 m (1 ⅛ yds) cotton edging lace,
   1 cm (½ in) wide
Bias binding
40 cm (16 in) narrow elastic
Lace collar
3 small pearl buttons

Cutting out
1. Trace the patterns for the yokes
and the sleeve on pages 151–154. Cut
out two pieces of fabric, each
measuring 33 cm x 115 cm (13 in x
45 in), for the front and back of the
skirt. From the remaining fabric cut
out two front yokes, four back yokes,
two sleeves, two ties (each measuring
9 cm x 55 cm [3 ½ in x 22 in]) and
four strips for the frill (each
measuring 9 cm x 115 cm [3 ½ in x
45 in]). Set one front yoke and two
back yokes aside for the lining.

Smocking

2. Adjust the needles of the smocking pleater to half spacing, or use smocking dots, and prepare the front section of the skirt for smocking (*see* page 25). Pull up ten rows of pleats. Do not smock the top and bottom rows of pleats. The smocking design is worked on the centre eight rows of pleats. Complete the smocking following Fig. 110c, which illustrates the eight rows of the smocking design. Set the pleats (*see* page 29). Remove the gathering threads.

Attaching yokes to skirt sections

3. With right sides together, pin the front yoke to the smocked section of the skirt, matching centres and small dots. Tack and machine stitch, using an overlock stitch, or a straight stitch and then a zigzag stitch. Trim the seam and press it up.

4. Make a placket in the skirt back (*see* page 42) and gather the top edge of both sections of the skirt back (*see* page 42). With right sides together, pin the two sections of the skirt back to the back yokes, placing the two edges of the placket as shown in Fig. 110b. Pull up the gathers to fit, then tack and machine stitch using an overlock stitch, or a straight and then a zigzag stitch. Press the seams up.

Shoulder seams

5. With right sides together, stitch the front to the back at the shoulders. Press the seams open. Stay-stitch around the neck opening.

Making and attaching the yoke lining

6. With right sides together, stitch the front yoke to the back yokes at the shoulders. Press the seams open. Stay-stitch around the neck edge. Fold 1 cm (½ in) to the wrong side along the lower edge of the front and back yokes. Press. With right sides together, pin the lining to the yoke around the neck and down the centre back edges. Tack and then machine

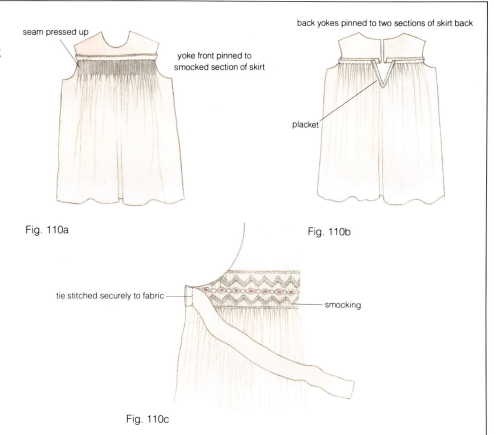

seam pressed up
yoke front pinned to smocked section of skirt

Fig. 110a

back yokes pinned to two sections of skirt back
placket

Fig. 110b

tie stitched securely to fabric
smocking

Fig. 110c

stitch around the neck and down the centre back edges. Stitch the neck edge a second time to strengthen it. Trim the seam to neaten, clip across the corners and clip the curves of the neck edge. Turn the lining to the inside and press. Tack the armhole edges together. Pin the lower edges of the lining to the stitching line of the front and back seams, so that the lining covers the seams. Tack and slip-stitch in place.

Sleeves

7. Along the lower edge of both sleeves turn 5 mm (¼ in) and then a further 5 mm (¼ in) to the wrong side, then pin, tack and machine stitch. On the right side, pin the wrong side of the edging lace to the lower edge of the sleeves along the straight edge with the scallops of the lace facing outwards, then tack and machine stitch carefully, close to the straight edge of the lace, using a straight stitch.

8. To make the casing for the elastic, pin the bias binding, folds down, to the wrong side of the sleeves in the

position marked on the sleeve pattern. Tack and stitch close to both edges of each casing. Cut two pieces of elastic, each the child's arm measurement plus 3 cm (1 ¼ in), thread the elastic through the casings and stitch the ends to the fabric.

9. At the top of the sleeves, stitch along the seam line, and just inside the seam line, between the small dots, using very long machine stitches. Do not pull up the gathers until the sleeves are in position.

Setting sleeves into armholes

10. With right sides together, pin the sleeve to the armhole edge, matching the large dot with the shoulder seam, and matching the small dots of the sleeve and the armhole edge. Pull up the gathers at the top of the sleeve to fit the armhole. Pin, tack and machine stitch, using an overlock stitch or a straight stitch and then a zigzag stitch. Repeat for second sleeve.

Making the ties

11. Fold each of the ties in half lengthways and, with right sides together, pin, tack and machine stitch along one long side and one short side of each tie. Clip across the corners, turn the ties the right way out, and press. Pin the unstitched end of the ties to the front skirt just below the armholes, and tack in place.

Completing the side seams

12. Stitch the entire side seam (from the inside edge of the sleeve to the lower edge of the skirt) in one continuous seam, using a French seam (*see* page 43). Stitch the second side seam in exactly the same way. Make sure that the ties are securely stitched into the side seams.

Making and attaching the frill

13. Cut the selvedges off the four strips of fabric and join the strips along their short sides, using French seams. Press the seams open. Make a narrow hem along the lower edge of the frill by turning back 5 mm (¼ in) and then a further 5 mm (¼ in). Pin, tack and machine stitch, using a straight stitch. Gather the top edge of the frill (*see* page 42). Place the right sides together and match the four seams of the frill with the two side seams, the centre front and the centre back of the dress. Pin the top edge of the frill to the lower edge of the dress. Pull up the gathers to fit, tack and machine stitch using an overlock stitch or a straight stitch and then a zigzag stitch. Remove tacking threads.

Attaching the collar

14. Fold the neck edge of the lace collar just to the inside of the neck edge of the yoke and carefully pin it in place, then tack and stitch by hand using a small running stitch.

Completing the dress

15. Sew the buttons to the right-hand back bodice, spacing them evenly. On the left-hand back bodice make three button loops with buttonhole stitch (*see* page 43) that are large enough for a button to pass through, to correspond with the three buttons.

A pretty, smocked pinafore worn over an old-fashioned 'granny-print' dress.

CHILD'S PINAFORE

This lacy pinafore looks particularly charming worn over a smocked dress like the one featured on page 96, or an old-fashioned 'granny-print' dress.

Requirements
75 cm (29 ½ in) cotton, lawn or
   muslin, 115 cm (45 in) wide
Tracing paper
Water-soluble pen
Matching thread
4 m (4 ⅜ yds) cotton insertion lace,
   2.5 cm (1 in) wide
1.10 m (1 ⅕ yds) cotton edging lace,
   1 cm (½ in) wide
3 small pearl buttons

Cutting out
1. From the 115 cm (45 in) wide cotton fabric cut out a rectangle measuring 47 cm x 115 cm (18 ½ in x 45 in) for the skirt and set aside.

2. Trace off the patterns for the bodice front and back on pages 155–156 . Cut the pattern pieces out.

3. Pin the pattern pieces for the two halves of the bodice back and the front to the remaining fabric and trace around them. Mark the position of the insertion lace on the bodice front, then remove the pattern pieces. Before cutting out, stay-stitch around all bodice sections, close to the outside edge of the seam allowance, to prevent fraying. Cut out the back bodice pieces.

Bodice front

4. Wash and iron the lace (*see* page 38). Before cutting out the bodice front, cut the strips of insertion lace, slightly longer than required. Pin these strips to the bodice front, then tack and carefully machine stitch, using a straight stitch, along both edges of each strip of lace. Now cut out the bodice front. Working on the wrong side, carefully cut away the fabric behind each of the strips, leaving 6 mm (¼ in) of fabric inside the stitching with which to make a neat hem. To make these tiny hems, turn back 3 mm (⅛ in) and then another 3 mm (⅛ in), and finger-press. Tack and stitch each hem neatly by hand.

Shoulder seams

5. Stitch the bodice front to the two halves of the back at the shoulder, using French seams (*see* page 43).

Bodice back

6. On the centre back edge of both halves of the bodice back, turn under 5 mm (¼ in) and another 1 cm (½ in). Pin, tack and slip-stitch. Make a narrow hem on the neck and armhole edges by turning under 2 mm (⅛ in) and then a further 3 mm (⅛ in). Finger-press, tack and neatly stitch these hems by hand.

Neck edge

7. Cut the narrow edging lace into three strips, one measuring 40 cm (16 in) and two measuring 35 cm (14 in) each. To finish off the neck, carefully gather the edge of the 40 cm (16 in) strip (*see* page 39) so that it measures 27 cm (10 ½ in). Make a hem at each end of the lace by turning under 3 mm (⅛ in) and then 3 mm (⅛ in) and slip-stitching. With right sides together, pin the gathered edge of the lace to the neck edge and tack and slip-stitch in place.

Armhole edges

8. To finish off the armhole edges, gather the long straight edges of both

the 35 cm (14 in) strips of lace so that each measures 26 cm (10 in). With right sides together, pin one strip of lace to one armhole edge, tack and neatly stitch in place. Attach the second strip to the other armhole edge in the same way.

Bodice side seams

9. Join the bodice side seams using French seams (*see* page 43).

Pinafore skirt

10. Lay the rectangle of fabric set aside for the skirt on a table and draw three parallel lines horizontally across it, at the following distances from the bottom edge of the fabric: 8.5 cm (3 ¼ in), 15 cm (6 in) and 21.5 cm (8 ½ in).

11. From the remaining insertion lace, cut three strips, each measuring 115 cm (45 in) in length. Pin the three strips of insertion lace along the three horizontal lines, placing the bottom edge of each strip on the line, then gently smooth the lace upwards and pin the top edge of each strip to the fabric. Tack and carefully machine stitch using a straight stitch, along both edges of each strip of lace. Turn the fabric to the wrong side, and carefully cut away the material behind

each strip, leaving 6 mm (¼ in) of fabric inside each line of stitching. Make tiny hems by folding back 3 mm (⅛ in) and then 3 mm (⅛ in) and finger-pressing. Tack and stitch each hem neatly by hand.

12. Make a hem along both side edges of the fabric by folding 5 mm (¼ in) and a further 1 cm (½ in) to the wrong side; pin, tack and hem neatly by hand.

13. Make a wider hem along the bottom edge of the skirt by turning under 5 mm (¼ in) and then 4 cm (1 ½ in); pin, tack and hem by hand.

14. Gather the top edge of the fabric (*see* page 42) and pull up the gathers to fit the bottom edge of the bodice. Join the skirt to the bodice using a French seam (*see* page 43).

Finishing off

15. Sew three little pearl buttons to the right-hand back bodice, spacing them evenly. On the left-hand back bodice, embroider three button loops using buttonhole stitch (*see* page 43) that are large enough for a button to pass through, to correspond with the three buttons. Remove all tacking threads.

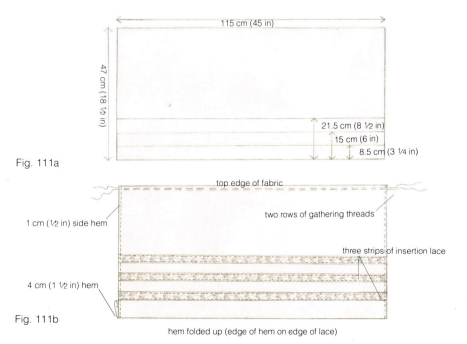

Fig. 111a

Fig. 111b

hem folded up (edge of hem on edge of lace)

FABRIC DOOR GARLAND

Requirements

5 m (5 ½ yds) colourfast red or tartan
   fabric, 12 cm (4 ¾ in) wide
Thread to match fabric
5 m (5 ½ yds) white or cream nylon
   lace, 2 ½ cm (1 in) wide
Thread to match lace
5 m (5 ½ yds) green or tartan ribbon
Thread to match ribbon
One 30 cm (12 in) embroidery hoop
1 m (1 ⅛ yd) ribbon to tie into a
   double bow
2 glass bells, or other ornaments
14 cm (5 ½ in) silver or gold thread
32 cm (12 ½ in) narrow green ribbon
   to make a loop

Making up

If you would like your garland to have a
very stiff frill, use spray-on starch while
ironing the fabric.

1. Make a small, neat hem along one
long edge of the fabric, using a
narrow hemming foot (*see* page 9), or
turn back 5 mm (¼ in) and then a
further 5 mm (¼ in) and pin, tack and
stitch using a straight stitch. (If two or
more strips of fabric need to be
joined, make a narrow hem on each
strip first, before joining them
together using French seams—*see*
page 43.) Do not cut off the selvedges
at either end of the 5 m (5 ½ yds) frill,
as hems are too bulky. For the same
reason, overlock the other long edge
of the frill, or use a straight stitch and
then a zigzag stitch. Trim away any
ragged threads.

2. Fold back 3 cm (1 ¼ in) to the
wrong side of the fabric, along the
overlocked or zigzagged edge, to form
a casing. Pin, tack and machine stitch
neatly using a straight stitch.

MAKING A DOUBLE OR MULTIPLE BOW

Requirements (for a double bow,
measuring 12 cm (4 ¾ in) across)
55 cm (22 in) narrow satin ribbon
   (each extra circle of ribbon will
   require a further 27.5 cm (11 in))
38 cm (15 in) matching ribbon for
   double streamers
Florists' wire

Making up

1. Hold one end of the 55cm (22 in)
length of ribbon between thumb and
forefinger of the left hand and make
two circles of ribbon about 12 cm
(4 ¾ in) in diameter, around your
fingers, one on top of the other.

2. With the thumb and forefinger of
both hands press the top and bottom
of the two circles of ribbon together so
that they resemble a bow and gently
twist the remaining ribbon around the
meeting point of the top and bottom
of the circles. To secure the bow, fold a
short length of florists' wire around
the twisted centre, bringing the ends
of the wire to the back of the bow and
twist them together tightly. Cut off the
excess wire with wirecutters.

3. Fold the 38 cm (15 in) length of
ribbon in half and cut it into two equal
lengths. Place matching halves
together, fold them in half again and
secure in the centre with florists' wire.
Cut off the excess wire. Cut
swallowtails at the end of each of the
four streamers. Stick the streamers to
whatever project you are decorating
and stick the centre of the bow to the
centre of the streamers with the
all-purpose glue.

3. With the scallops facing outwards,
pin the wrong side of the lace, close
to the edge of the right side of the
frill, then tack and machine stitch
neatly using a straight stitch. Pin one
edge of the tartan or green ribbon so
that it slightly overlaps the straight
edge of the lace, or leave a gap of
1.5 cm (⅝ in) between the edge of the
ribbon and the straight edge of the
lace. Tack and machine stitch close to
both edges of the ribbon.

4. Separate the inner and outer rings
of the embroidery hoop. Using a
sharp knife, carefully cut the inner
ring of the hoop, and push one of the
the cut ends of the wooden ring
through the casing. Arrange the
pleats evenly around the hoop and
then push both ends of the inner ring
into the opposite ends of the casing
for about 1 cm (½ in), so that the
ends of the ring overlap each other
inside the casing.

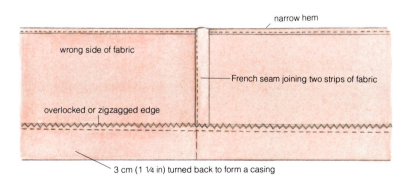

narrow hem
wrong side of fabric
French seam joining two strips of fabric
overlocked or zigzagged edge
3 cm (1 ¼ in) turned back to form a casing

Fig. 112

5. Replace the outer ring of the hoop and tighten the screw.

6. Cut the ribbon for the bow into two halves. Place them together, fold them in half, and tie a knot. Stick the knot to the front edge of the outer ring just below the screw. Make a double bow with the ribbon (*see* page 10) and stick the bow to the knot. Tie the two bells (or other ornaments) to the loose ends of the gold or silver thread, and knot the thread around the screw. Make a loop from the 32 cm (12 ½ in) of green ribbon and sew the loop to the back of the frill just above the screw. The frill can easily be removed from the wooden ring for laundering if necessary.

LACE WINDOW DECORATION

Delicately candlewicked Lace Window Decoration (this page), filled with pot-pourri.

This pretty window decoration is filled with pot-pourri. As the sun shines through the window and the decoration, the pot-pourri will become warm and its scent will fill the whole room, and it will look lovely with the bright colours showing through the embroidered muslin.

Requirements
30 cm x 30 cm (12 in x 12 in) fine muslin or voile for the front
Water-soluble pen
25 cm (10 in) embroidery hoop
Crochet cotton or embroidery thread
2 m (2 ¼ yds) lace of desired width
Matching thread
All-purpose glue
30 cm x 30 cm (12 in x 12 in) fine muslin or voile for the backing
Brightly coloured pot-pourri
Silver or gold thread or ribbon

Making up
1. Fold one 30 cm x 30 cm (12 in x 12 in) piece of muslin in half vertically and then in half horizontally. Finger-press. Open out the fabric and match the centre lines of the fabric with those of the design on page 157. Trace the design on to the fabric.

2. Place the fabric in the hoop and pull it taut. Candlewick or embroider the design using desired thread.

3. Wash and iron the completed design very well (*see* page 14), then replace it in the hoop.

4. Draw a line close to and around the bottom edge of the hoop. Remove the fabric from the hoop and draw another line 6 mm (¼ in) away from the first, around the circumference. Trim away the excess fabric.

5. Wash and iron the lace (*see* page 38) and gather it (*see* page 39) until it measures 71 cm (28 in). Join the two short ends of the lace together using a French seam (*see* page 43).

6. With right sides together (and the scalloped edge of the lace lying towards the centre of the circle), pin the straight edge of the gathered lace to the raw edge of the circle. Tack and then machine stitch, using an overlock stitch, or a straight stitch and then a zigzag stitch. Trim away any ragged threads and remove tacking stitches.

7. Spread glue all the way around the outer edge of the inner wooden hoop. Stretch the square of muslin for the back across the back and up the outer edge of the same hoop. Press the fabric against the glue firmly, and allow the glue to dry. Trim away all the excess fabric carefully. Turn the right way up and fill with pot-pourri.

8. Centre the embroidered circle over the inner wooden hoop. Replace the outer wooden hoop and tighten the screw securely. Pull the fabric fairly taut and adjust the lace ruffles so that they will lie flat when the decoration is hung against the window.

9. Sew a loop of thread or ribbon to the back of the lace frill, to make a loop from which to hang the decoration.

LACE FAN TREE DECORATION

Requirements

25 cm (10 in) lace, 5 cm (2 in) wide
Matching thread
Thin, stiff cardboard
All-purpose glue
32 cm (12 ½ in) narrow ribbon
28 cm (11 in) narrow ribbon for a
     double bow
Dried flowers (optional)
12 cm (4 ¾ in) narrow ribbon for loop

Making up

1. Wash, starch and iron the lace (*see* page 38). Fold the lace into neat pleats using the scallops on the edge of the lace as a guide. Secure the pleats at the base of the fan by neatly stitching through all the pleats several times, as close to the end of the pleats as possible.

2. Open out the fan. Cut the cardboard to the length of the straight edge of the fan, and a width of 5 mm (¼ in). Stick the straight edge of the fan to the cardboard.

3. Cut the 32 cm (12 ½ in) length of ribbon in half. Place the two pieces of ribbon together, fold them in half and make a knot. Stitch the knot to the centre of the base of the fan. Make a small double bow (*see* page 101) with the 28 cm (11 in) length of ribbon. Stick the bow to the knot. Make a small posy of dried flowers and stick this to the centre of the bow.

4. Fold the 12 cm (4 ¾ in) length of ribbon to make a loop. Glue the two ends of the ribbon together. Sew or stick the loop to the centre back of the fan.

lace folded into tight pleats   small posy of flowers

double satin ribbon bow

Fig. 113

LACE HEART

Requirements

2 pipe-cleaners
1 m (1 ⅛ yds) eyelet lace
All-purpose glue
12 cm (4 ¾ in) narrow ribbon for a
     loop
28 cm (11 in) narrow ribbon for a
     double bow
Small posy of dried flowers

Making up

1. Place two pipe-cleaners together and twist their bottom ends together to join them.

2. Fold the lace in half, and mark the halfway point with a pin. Beginning at the halfway mark, weave the right pipe-cleaner in and out through the holes along the straight edge of the right-hand half of the lace. Simultaneously, push the left pipe-cleaner through the holes along the straight edge of the left-hand half of the lace (*see* Fig. 114). Once all the lace has been threaded on to the pipe-cleaners, twist the two loose ends of the pipe-cleaners together.

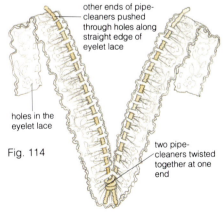

other ends of pipe-cleaners pushed through holes along straight edge of eyelet lace

holes in the eyelet lace

Fig. 114

two pipe-cleaners twisted together at one end

3. Bend the pipe-cleaners into a heart shape. Ensure that the pointed end has enough gathers to form a neat fan shape. Glue a loop of narrow ribbon to the back of the heart. Make a single or double bow from the 28 cm (11 in) length of ribbon (*see* page 101) and glue it to the front. Glue the posy of dried flowers to the centre of the bow, facing downwards.

Lace Fan Tree Decorations and Lace Hearts (both this page) in an elegant green and white Christmas setting.

LACY HANDKERCHIEF CHRISTMAS CRACKER

If filled with pot-pourri or little gifts, these make wonderful, dainty presents for all manner of special occasions.

Requirements

9 cm x 11 cm (3 ½ in x 4 in) thin, white cardboard
All-purpose glue
Lace-edged handkerchief
Spray-on starch
90 cm (35 ½ in) white ribbon or lace, approximately 1 cm (½ in) wide
Small gifts or pot-pourri
Gypsophila or other dried flowers

Making up

1. Bend the cardboard to form a tube and stick one long edge to the other.

2. Starch the handkerchief using spray-on starch, and iron carefully. Place the handkerchief on a flat surface. Place the cardboard tube on the edge of the handkerchief and roll it carefully to form a tube. The lace edge of the handkerchief should lie on the underside of the tube. Tie a length of ribbon around one end of the handkerchief, close to the end of the tube. Finish with a pretty bow. Put the gift or pot-pourri inside the cardboard tube before tying the second bow at the other end.

3. Tuck dried flowers under the knot of each bow.

Lacy Handkerchief Christmas Crackers and Lace Coasters (both this page).

HINT *Push a cardboard tube carefully into each end of the cracker to force out the creases made when tying the bows and to make the ends of the cracker look nice and round, and then remove.*

LACE COASTERS

Making these pretty lace coasters is a handy way to use up fairly small bits of linen and lace that are too precious to throw away. Given in sets of six, they make wonderful gifts.

Requirements (for each coaster)

Tracing paper
Water-soluble pen
7.5 cm x 7.5 cm (3 in x 3 in) linen square
2 pieces of lace, each 3.5 cm x 7.5 cm (1 ¼ in x 3 in)
Matching thread

Making up

1. Trace the pattern for the coaster on page 159 on to tracing paper and then on to the linen; cut out the linen base of the coaster.

edges of two pieces of lace placed close together

overlocked edges

Fig. 116

2. Position the lace as shown in Fig. 116. Pin, tack, and, using a narrow overlock stitch, or a straight stitch and then a zigzag stitch, stitch all the way round the outside edge. Trim away any untidy threads.

side view of bow

Fig. 115

lace edge placed at the base of the cracker

LACE FAN

Buy a pretty, cheap fan and transform it into a beautiful lace fan that will make a useful and decorative gift.

Determining the length of lace required

Measure the top arc of the fabric or paper in the existing fan when it is completely open. Add 1 cm (½ in) to this measurement to allow 5 mm (¼ in) to turn under at either end. Measure from top to bottom to determine the width of the lace required.

Requirements

Fan with wooden framework
Fine cotton lace of required size
Glue that will not mark the lace

Making up

1. Soak the fan in plain, warm water to remove the fabric. Clean the existing glue off the spokes (some fans have water-soluble glue, which is easily wiped off), and wipe the framework dry. Allow it to dry completely.

2. Place the framework on a flat surface like an ironing board, so that pins may be pressed vertically into the surface to keep the spokes in position. Spread the framework out into a fan shape and arrange the spokes so that they are equidistant. Place a pin on either side of each spoke so that they do not move.

3. On the left-hand edge of the lace, turn under 5 mm (¼ in); on the right-hand edge of the lace turn 5 mm (¼ in) towards the right side of the lace (so that it will be correctly positioned for gluing) and carefully glue in place.

4. Spread the glue very thinly on the upper side of the spokes, and on the two ends. Carefully stick the lace to the spokes.

DOILY CONE

Requirements

1 crocheted or embroidered doily, 10–12 cm (4–4 ¾ in) in diameter
Spray-on starch
15 cm (6 in) matching or contrasting ribbon, 1 cm (½ in) wide
Matching thread
45 cm (18 in) ribbon, as above
Dried flowers or sweets

Making up

1. Wash the doily (*see* page 38) and then starch with spray-on starch. Iron the doily dry. Starch and iron the short length of ribbon, which will be made into a handle.

2. Fold the doily (*see* Fig. 117a). Beginning where the folds meet, thread the longer length of narrow ribbon through the holes around the top edge of the cone, leaving approximately 15 cm (6 in) of ribbon hanging loose at each end. Tie a pretty bow and cut a swallowtail (V-shape) into the ends of the ribbon.

Fig. 117a

3. Stitch the two folds of the doily together (*see* Fig. 117b). Neatly stitch the ribbon handle into place. Fill with dried flowers or sweets.

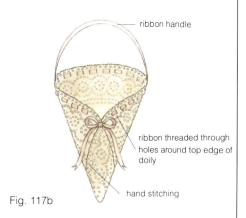

ribbon handle

ribbon threaded through holes around top edge of doily

hand stitching

Fig. 117b

Lace Fan (this page), Victorian Handkerchief Sachets (page 107), and Pretty Pot-pourri Sachets (page 107) — all make lovely gifts.

POT-POURRI AND DRIED FLOWERS

The very thought of pot-pourri recalls many happy memories of a wonderful childhood. I grew up on a smallholding on which my parents grew flowers for the markets and various florists. There were over 5,000 rose bushes, which were a magnificent sight when in bloom, and large areas of carnations and sweet peas. My first attempts at making pot-pourri (without a recipe) as a small child were a disaster. I remember following my father around as he 'dead-headed' the rosebushes and picking up baskets full of open roses, and being terribly upset because my 'pot-pourri' went mouldy. Nobody had told me that the flowers had to be carefully dried first!

There is nothing mysterious about making pot-pourri. All you need to do is to follow these easy instructions and use a little imagination.

Pot-pourri should contain flowers and herbs, spices, fixatives and essential oil. Pot-pourri recipes can usually be adapted and you can replace any of the ingredients with a similar ingredient in the same category.

A simple recipe for pot-pourri has been included here because many of the projects, such as cushions, sachets and Christmas decorations, can be stuffed with pot-pourri.

FLOWERS SUITABLE FOR MAKING POT-POURRI

Roses (particularly red, dark pink, yellow and orange), carnations, bougainvillaea, larkspur, delphiniums, peonies, lavender, gypsophila, honesty, fuschia, calendula, hydrangea, anemone, clove pinks, marigolds, stocks, jonquil, sweet peas, agapanthus, pansy and cornflower.

HERBS AND LEAVES SUITABLE FOR MAKING POT-POURRI
Scented leaves

Mint (eau-de-cologne, peppermint, spearmint and ordinary garden mint), lemon balm, lemon verbena, marjoram, basil, sage, lavender, rosemary, bergamot, bay leaves, southernwood, scented geranium (rose, lemon, and peppermint) and small citrus leaves.

Unscented leaves

Rose, ivy, conifer sprigs, various ferns, any small or medium-sized leaf that looks attractive and lichens.

SEEDS AND SEEDPODS SUITABLE FOR MAKING POT-POURRI

Seeds and seedpods add interest and texture to pot-pourri.

Good examples are cotoneaster and hawthorn berries, different types of rosehips, acorns, tiny citrus fruits, pine tree buds, small pine-cones, various seedpods, Chinese lanterns, love-in-a-mist and poppy heads.

FIXATIVES

Fixatives include: orris root, gum benzoin, citrus peel (dried), tonquin beans, vetiver, spices and oak moss (a type of lichen).

Most spices can be used as fixatives. Some examples are: nutmeg, cinnamon, allspice, coriander, vanilla, cloves, ginger and star anise. Use whole spices that have been freshly ground in a grinder.

HARVESTING AND DRYING

All flowers, leaves and herbs must be absolutely dry before they are picked, so pick them on a dry day after the dew has evaporated, but before the sun becomes too hot, as the sap rises and the essential oil evaporates. They may also be picked in the afternoon before the dew falls. Herbs should be harvested before they bloom.

Drying whole flowers

Remove the leaves from the stalks, so that the air can circulate between the stalks properly. Tie the flowers or sprigs of herbs into small bunches and hang them upside-down in a warm, dry place (but not in direct sunlight), such as a kitchen, attic or airing cupboard, until they are quite dry.

Drying petals and herbs

Remove all the petals and leaves from the stems and spread them out in a single layer on a clean sheet or piece of newspaper, away from direct sunlight.

Remember to turn them over from time to time to prevent them from becoming mouldy. When dry (drying can take anything from 24 hours to three weeks, depending on the weather) store them in airtight containers (preferably glass), in a warm, dry place.

POT-POURRI RECIPE

The following basic recipe is very easy and the variations are endless:

Requirements

3 cups of dried rose petals and a few dried whole roses
1 cup dried rose leaves
2 cups dried lavender florets and several dried whole flowers
1 cup (or more if you prefer) dried herbs such as lemon verbena, mint or rose geranium
2 tablespoons spices — cloves, cinnamon and allspice in equal quantities
2 tablespoons orris root, or any other fixative
5–10 drops essential oil (rose, carnation or violet)

1. Mix all the dried petals and herbs in a large glass or pottery bowl.

2. In a separate container, mix the fixatives, spices and oil together thoroughly. Then add this mixture to the petals.

3. Mix thoroughly once again, then store the mixture in airtight containers for four to six weeks. Shake the containers frequently during the storage time.

Do not throw away any faded, ugly pot-pourri. Instead, revive it by adding more spice and oil, store in a sealed container for a day or two, and use this to fill cushions, tea cosy pockets, sachets or any projects in which it will not be visible.

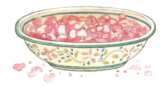

PRETTY POT-POURRI SACHETS

You may have inherited small linen, lace, cotton and crocheted articles that are very beautiful, but rather a nuisance to launder. Coasters, doilies and various other small articles made of lace can be transformed into beautiful sachets and filled with sweet-smelling pot-pourri (*see* the recipe on page 106). These sachets can be placed inside pillowslips, drawers and linen cupboards, or even hung from a little loop of ribbon on door and drawer handles, to give a fresh garden fragrance to your linen, clothes or any room in the house.

Requirements
1 lace coaster or doily
Spray-on starch (optional)
A saucer
Cotton fabric to match the coaster or doily, enough to cut out 2 circles the same size
Water-soluble pen
Matching thread
A generous handful of pot-pourri
50 cm (20 in) satin ribbon for a bow and a loop (optional)

Making up
1. Wash and iron the coaster or doily carefully (*see* page 38) and, if necessary, starch it so that it looks crisp.

2. Find an object the same size as the doily (for example, a perfectly round saucer), around which you can trace a circle. Trace off and cut out two circles of cotton fabric.

3. Pin and tack the two circles of fabric together. Sew around the circumference using an overlock stitch, or a straight and then a zigzag stitch. Leave a 6 cm (2 ¼ in) opening.

4. Turn the little sachet the right way out. With a blunt object, ease the

seam so that the sachet is perfectly round. Press using a damp cloth. Making sure that it is dry, fill the sachet with pot-pourri, lavender, lemon verbena or any other sweet-smelling herb. Slip-stitch the opening closed.

5. Carefully pin the sachet to the underside of the doily, centring it properly. Tack and hand or machine stitch around the edge of the sachet.

6. Make a pretty single or double satin ribbon bow (*see* page 101), and stitch it to the doily by hand. Sew a loop of ribbon to the back of the sachet if you wish to hang it from a door-handle, drawer-knob, bed-knob or coat-hanger.

VARIATION
Thread the satin ribbon through the holes around the outside edge of the doily—this looks particularly pretty if the doily is knitted or crocheted—and leave a length of ribbon hanging loose at the beginning and the end. Tie a pretty bow with the ends.

VICTORIAN HANDKERCHIEF SACHET

Have you ever wondered what to do with those beautiful lace-edged, hand-embroidered handkerchiefs? It seems a pity to leave them tucked away in a drawer or cupboard. The Victorians used squares of muslin or lawn to make sachets that they pinned to the backs of chairs, and into the folds of curtains, so that as they drew the curtains a wonderful fragrance filled the air. Handkerchiefs may be used to make pretty sachets in the same way, and are attractive enough to be seen pinned to the backs of chairs or displayed on a mantelpiece. They also make a lovely gift for any lady, young or old.

Pretty Pot-pourri Sachet (this page).

Requirements
1 lacy handkerchief
Spray-on starch (optional)
A good handful of pot-pourri
35 cm (14 in) narrow satin ribbon

Making up
1. Wash and iron the handkerchief very well (*see* page 14). If the fabric is limp, spray it with spray-on starch as you are ironing it.

2. Spread the handkerchief out on a flat surface, and place the pot-pourri in the centre of the handkerchief. Have the piece of ribbon at hand.

3. Bring the corners of the handkerchief together, and hold them with one hand; with the other hand, gather the folds into a 'waist' just above the pot-pourri. Let go of the four corners and, with the same hand, wind the ribbon around the 'waist'. Now, with both hands free, tie a bow. Adjust the folds.

HINT An *ideal way to make use of small scraps of lace that are too pretty to throw away is to carefully cut out the motifs from the pieces of lace, and to stitch these by hand to all sorts of articles, such as sachets, cushions, towels, tablecloths, bed linen and articles of clothing.*

CINNAMON DECORATION

Requirements

4 cinnamon sticks
30 cm (12 in) red, green or tartan
    ribbon
All-purpose glue
Extra ribbon for bows (optional)

Making up

Tie the four cinnamon sticks tightly together with the ribbon, tie a knot and make a loop by gluing the two ends of the ribbon together.

CONE WREATH

Requirements

Selection of small cones, seeds and
    seedpods, acorns, rosehips, poppy
    heads, ginger, nutmeg and short
    lengths of cinnamon stick
Polystyrene or dry foam ring, 20 cm
    (8 in) in diameter
All-purpose glue

Making up

Choose an interesting selection from the above list and stick them to the polystyrene ring using all-purpose glue, following the manufacturer's instructions carefully. Fill in gaps between cones or other objects with smaller seeds or poppy heads.

Fig. 118

Cinnamon Decorations (this page), Small Willow Wreath (this page), Patchwork Balls (page 111), Pinecone Father Christmases (page 110), and a Red Poinsettia (page 110).

SMALL WILLOW OR VINE WREATH

Requirements

Long willow or vine fronds
Florists' wire
Ribbon
All-purpose glue
Tiny cones, pepper berries, tiny poppy
    heads, small gold or silver beads,
    small dried flowers

Making up

1. With one hand, hold on to one end of a very long, flexible willow or vine frond, and with the other hand bend the frond to form two or more circles of the same size; then wind the loose end of the frond around the circles to hold them together. Secure the loose end by winding the wire around it, and allow the wreath to dry out.

2. Beginning and ending at the top, wind the ribbon around the wreath and glue the ends of the ribbon together at the back of the wreath. Make a ribbon loop and stick it to the back of the wreath. Make a pretty bow (*see* page 101) and stick it to the front of the wreath, in whichever position you prefer. Now glue the cones, silver or gold beads, poppy heads and dried flowers to the front of the wreath.

DRIED FLOWER WREATH

Requirements
Florists' wire
Dried flowers, seedpods and cones
Dry florists' foam
80–90 cm (31 ½ –35 ½ in) wide
   satin ribbon

Making up
1. Cut the wire into 10 cm (4 in) lengths and bend about 3 cm (1 ¼ in) back on each length to form a 'shepherd's crook'.

2. Take small bunches of flowers and cut the stems to about 3 cm (1 ¼ in) in length. Place the bent end of the wire as close as possible to, and next to, the base of the flowers and wind the straight part of the wire around the bent end and the stems about three times. Straighten the rest of the wire so that it lies alongside the stems, and cut it to the correct length.

3. Select a few striking flowers to form focal points around the ring, wire them as described in Step 2, and push the wire stems into the foam ring, in the desired positions. Continue to add bunches of flowers,

until you have covered the whole of the foam ring. Any gaps may be filled in with small bunches of hydrangea, small pine-cones, poppy heads, gypsophila or anything else that you find pleasing.

4. Tie the satin ribbon into a pretty bow (*see* page 101), push one of the pieces of wire through the back of the bow, and twist the wire to secure. Place the bow in position.

5. Attach a loop made from the florists' wire to the ring (*see* Fig 120).

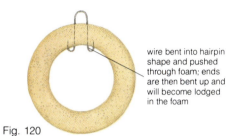

wire bent into hairpin shape and pushed through foam; ends are then bent up and will become lodged in the foam

Fig. 120

VARIATION
As a pretty variation to the round wreath, make a heart-shaped wreath.

Requirements (in addition to those listed above)
2 blocks of dry florists' foam
All-purpose glue
Tracing paper
Stiff cardboard
Sharp craft knife

Making up
1. Stick two blocks of foam together using glue and press together firmly.

2. Trace off the pattern on page 158, cut it out, and stick it on to stiff cardboard to make a template. Place the template on top of the two blocks, with the glue-line down the centre (*see* Fig. 121), and cut around the template with the craft knife. (The inner heart may be used to make a small, heart-shaped arrangement, for example, a candleholder.) Continue in the same manner as for the round wreath, following Steps 2–4.

   Two blocks of foam stuck together and cut in half will make two large and two small heart-shaped forms.

two blocks of florists' foam glued together

smaller inner heart

paper template on top of blocks (glue line down centre)

cutting line

glue line

Fig. 121

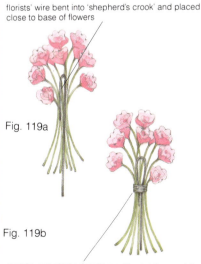

florists' wire bent into 'shepherd's crook' and placed close to base of flowers

Fig. 119a

Fig. 119b

straight end of 'shepherd's crook' wound around the bent end and stems of flowers

Detail of Dried Flower Wreath (variation, this page), Cone Wreath (page 108), Cinnamon Decorations (page 108), and Small Willow Wreath (page 108).

PINE-CONE FATHER CHRISTMAS

Requirements (for each Father Christmas)
Tracing paper
Thin, stiff cardboard
Red felt for hat
16 cm (6 ¼ in) very narrow red or
    green ribbon or silver thread
1 white or cream wooden bead,
    approximately the size of a marble
1 small pine-cone
All-purpose glue
Cotton wool for beard
Indelible marker pen for drawing
    the face

Making up
1. Trace the pattern for the Father
Christmas hat on page 159 on to
tracing paper, cut it out, and stick it
on to the cardboard.

2. Using this template, cut out a red
felt hat. On the short side of the
triangle, turn back 3 mm (⅛ in) to
form a rim. Stick the two long sides of
the triangle together to form a
pointed hat, but before you press the
two top edges together to form a
point, make a loop from the ribbon or
thread, knot the two ends together,
and insert the knotted ends into the
tip of the hat.

3. Stick the bead to the top of the
cone. Pull off a fairly large tuft of
cotton wool and stick this on to the
bead to form a beard. Draw a face on
the bead and stick the pointed hat to
the top of the bead.

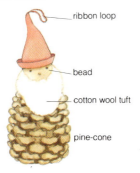

ribbon loop
bead
cotton wool tuft
pine-cone

Fig. 122

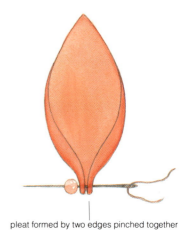

Red Poinsettia (*this page*) *being made, and complete.*

RED POINSETTIA

Requirements (for each flower)
Tracing paper
Thin, stiff cardboard
Red felt, 6.5 cm x 26 cm (2 ½ in x
    10 in) or 13 cm x 26 cm (5 in x
    10 in), if you wish to make very
    stiff petals
Spray-on starch (optional)
6.5 cm x 26 cm (2 ½ in x 10 in)
    iron-on fusible interfacing
    (optional)
Strong thread and needle
7 silver beads
14 cm (5 ½ in) narrow red or silver
    cord or ribbon
All-purpose glue

Making up
1. Trace the pattern for the petal on
page 159 on to tracing paper, cut it
out, and paste it on to the cardboard.

2. Stiffen the 26 cm x 6.5 cm (10 in x
2 ½ in) red felt using spray-on starch,
and then iron it; alternatively, if you
prefer stiffer petals, fold the 13 cm x
26 cm (5 in x 10 in) piece in half so
that it measures 6.5 cm x 26 cm
(2 ½ in x 10 in) and sandwich the
interfacing between the two layers of
the folded felt. Iron the felt using a
damp cloth so that the two layers of
felt will bond together.

3. Using the template, cut out seven
poinsettia petals from the felt. Thread
a needle using strong thread, then
double the thread and make a knot at
the end, leaving about 5 cm (2 in)
hanging loose.

4. At the blunt end of each petal,
pinch the two sides together to form a
pleat before pushing the needle and
thread through it (*see* Fig. 123). Pass
the needle alternately through petals
and silver beads. Once you have
threaded seven petals and seven
beads, pull the thread as tight as
possible and carefully knot the two
ends together several times; trim the
thread. Make a loop with the silver or
red ribbon or cord, and stick it to the
back of one of the petals.

pleat formed by two edges pinched together

Fig. 123

PATCHWORK BALL

Choose 'granny print' fabric with red, dark green, white or cream as the background colour. The other fabric should be plain.

Requirements

Tracing paper
Thin, stiff cardboard
All-purpose glue
10 cm (4 in) each of two or three different fabrics, 115 cm (45 in) wide (this will be sufficient for at least 6 balls)
2 pins per ball
Polystyrene balls, 8 cm (3 in) in diameter
Brightly coloured cotton thread
Very sharp razor blade or knife
50 cm (20 in) gold or silver ribbon, braid or ricrac (3–5 mm [1/8–1/4 in] wide) per ball

Cutting out

1. Trace off the template on page 159. Stick the template to the cardboard and cut it out. Fold the fabric carefully (*see* Fig. 124), and pin the template to the folded fabric. Trace around the template and cut out two of these segment shapes from each colour fabric (so that you have four segments), varying the colour combinations if you are making up several balls.

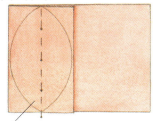

template pinned to folded fabric

Fig. 124

Dividing the ball into segments

2. Stick a pin into the top and bottom of the polystyrene ball (*see* Fig. 125). Twist one end of the thread around pin A and push the pin down tightly into the ball. Pull the thread down the side of the ball, twist it around pin B, and take it back up the opposite side of the ball to pin A. Twist the thread around pin A and repeat this procedure on the other side, so dividing the ball into four equal segments (*see* Fig. 125).

3. Cut a slit, 1 cm (1/2 in) deep, on one side of each of the four threads, using the threads as a guide. Be sure to join the slits at the top and bottom of the ball. Remove the threads and pins.

Covering the ball

4. Pin one of the fabric shapes over one of the segments, at the top and at the bottom (the fabric should be bigger than the segment). With the blunt edge of a knife, push the excess fabric into the slit on either side of the segment. Remove the pins and repeat the procedure on the opposite segment, using the same fabric. Cover the two remaining segments in the same way, using contrasting fabric. Neaten all the edges carefully and smooth away any creases.

Covering the slits

5. Fold the ribbon, braid or ricrac in half, but do not cut it. Pin the centre point of the ribbon, braid or ricrac to the ball at A and pull the two lengths down over the slits to B. Twist the two lengths so that they cross each other and bring them up on the opposite sides of the ball to A. In this way the spaces between the segments are covered. Carefully tie a neat knot (as close to the ball as possible) and make a loop by gluing the two loose ends together.

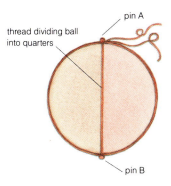

thread dividing ball into quarters
pin A
pin B

Fig. 125

Patchwork Balls (this page), covered in reds, greens and whites, in various stages of completion.

PINCUSHION

Requirements

1 small embroidered doily
Spray-on starch (optional)
1 saucer
Cotton fabric to match the doily,
    enough to cut out 2 circles the
    same size
Water-soluble pen
5 cm x 55 cm (2 in x 22 in) strip of
    cotton fabric, the same as above
Matching thread
Sawdust or polyester filling
Pot-pourri or lavender

Making up

1. Follow Steps 1 and 2 on page 107
for making a sachet with a doily.

2. Fold 6 mm (¼ in) to the wrong side
at both ends of the strip of fabric and

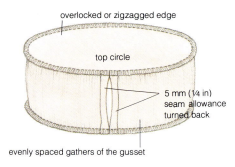

overlocked or zigzagged edge

top circle

5 mm (¼ in)
seam allowance
turned back

evenly spaced gathers of the gusset

Fig. 126

finger-press. Do not sew the short
ends of the strip of fabric together
yet, as they will be used as an
opening. Gather along both long
sides of the strip of fabric (*see* page
42) and pull up the gathers to fit
around the outside edge of one of the
circles of fabric. This strip will form a
gusset between the top and the
bottom of the pincushion.

3. With right sides together, pin the
gathered strip of fabric first to one
circle of fabric and then to the other
circle of fabric, adjusting the gathers
so that they are evenly spaced
(*see* Fig. 126). Leaving a small gap
through which to stuff the
pincushion, tack and then machine
stitch the three sections together,
using an overlock stitch, or a straight
and then a zigzag stitch.

4. Turn the little cushion shape the
right way out and stuff it with a
mixture of sawdust or polyester and
pot-pourri or lavender.

5. Slip-stitch the opening in the
gusset closed.

6. Follow Step 5 on page 107 for
making a sachet from a doily to
complete the pincushion.

A beautiful and unusual Pincushion (this page), made from a small embroidered doily.

· DESIGNS & PATTERNS ·

Although they refer to specific projects, most of the designs on the following pages can be used for embroidery, quilting or candlewicking. They can be reduced or enlarged and used to make an endless variety of projects.

Quilting design 1 for Quilted Bed Cover (page 50); *see* also page 117

Quilting design 2 for Quilted Bed Cover (page 50); *see* also page 117

Alternative quilting design 1 for Quilted Bed Cover (page 50); *see* also page 117

Alternative quilting design 2 for Quilted Bed Cover (page 50); *see* also page 117

Quilting design 1

Quilting design 2

Quilting design 1 (alternative)

Quilting design 2 (alternative)

Diagrams showing how quilting designs can be repeated and joined to form one continuous design.

The designs on the following pages have been halved. To recreate the full design, fold a piece of tracing paper in half vertically, and align the fold with the straight, vertical edge of the halved design. Trace the design, then turn the folded tracing paper over (again placing the fold on the vertical edge) and retrace the design on the other side.

Reduced designs have been provided as a guide.

Candlewick design for Candlewicked Quilt (pages 54–62)

Candlewick design for Candlewicked Quilt (pages 54–62)

Candlewick design for Candlewicked Quilt (pages 54–62)

Candlewick design for Candlewicked Quilt (pages 54–62)

Candlewick design for Candlewicked Quilt (pages 54–62)

Candlewick design for Candlewicked Quilt (pages 54–62)

Candlewick design for Candlewicked Quilt (pages 54–62)

Candlewick design for Candlewicked Quilt (pages 54–62)

Candlewick design for Candlewicked Quilt (pages 54–62)

Candlewick design for Candlewicked Quilt (pages 54–62)

Candlewick design for Candlewicked Quilt (pages 54–62)

Candlewick design for Candlewicked Quilt (pages 54–62)

Candlewick design for Candlewicked Quilt (pages 54–62)

Candlewick design for Candlewicked Quilt (pages 54–62)

Candlewick design for Candlewicked Quilt (pages 54–62)

Candlewick design for Candlewicked Quilt (pages 54–62)

Candlewick design for Candlewicked Quilt (pages 54–62); enlarge design to 140%

Candlewick design for Candlewicked Quilt (pages 54–62); enlarge design to 140%

Suggested arrangement of designs for Candlewicked Quilt (pages 54–62)

Nightdress Case (page 66)

Alternative design for Nightdress Case (page 66)

Alternative design for Nightdress Case (page 66)

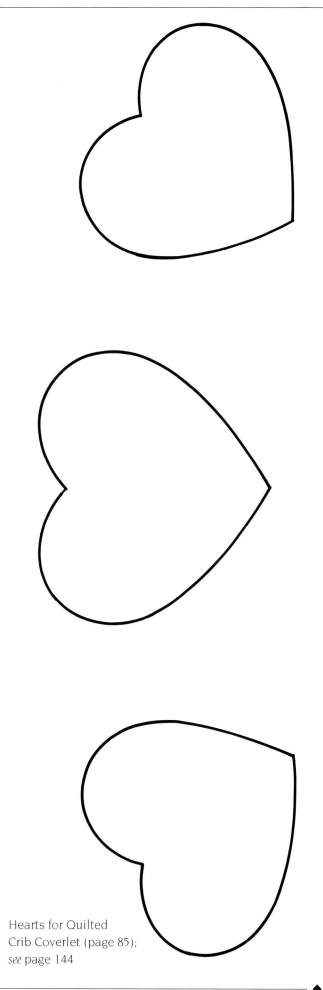

Hearts for Quilted
Crib Coverlet (page 85);
see page 144

Candlewicked Cushion (page 66)

Candlewicked Mirror Surround (page 68)

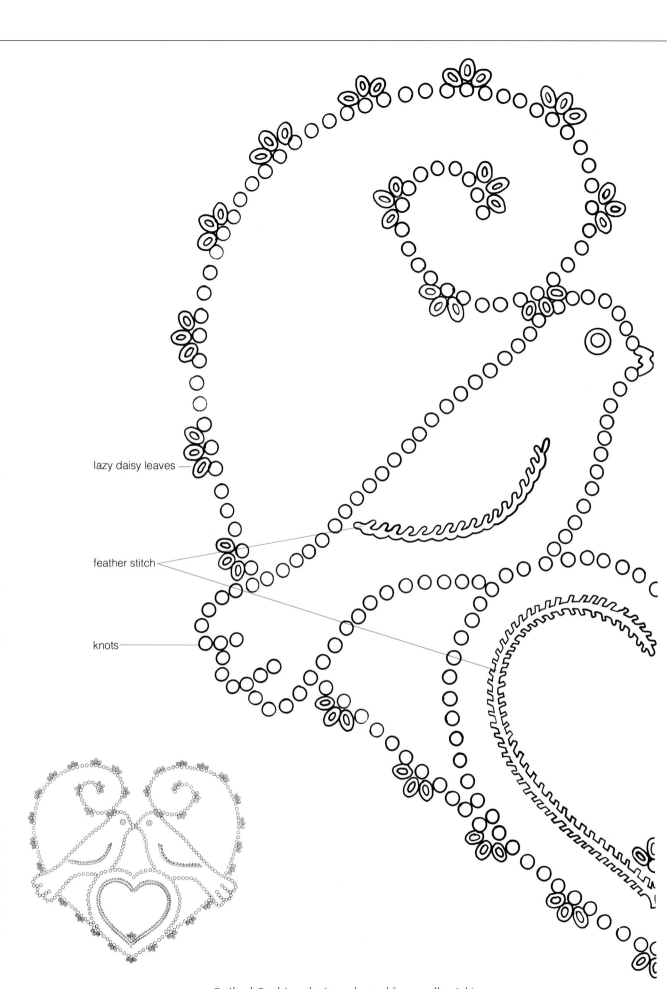

lazy daisy leaves —

feather stitch —

knots —

Quilted Cushion design adapted for candlewicking

Quilted Cushion (page 81)

Quilted Crib Coverlet (page 85); teddy bear design to be accompanied by hearts design on page 140

Italian quilting (see page 34) or candlewicking design

Design for Italian quilting (see page 34)

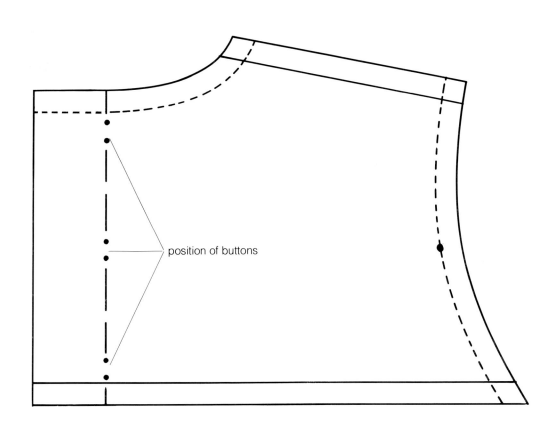

position of buttons

Christening Robe (page 93): back yoke

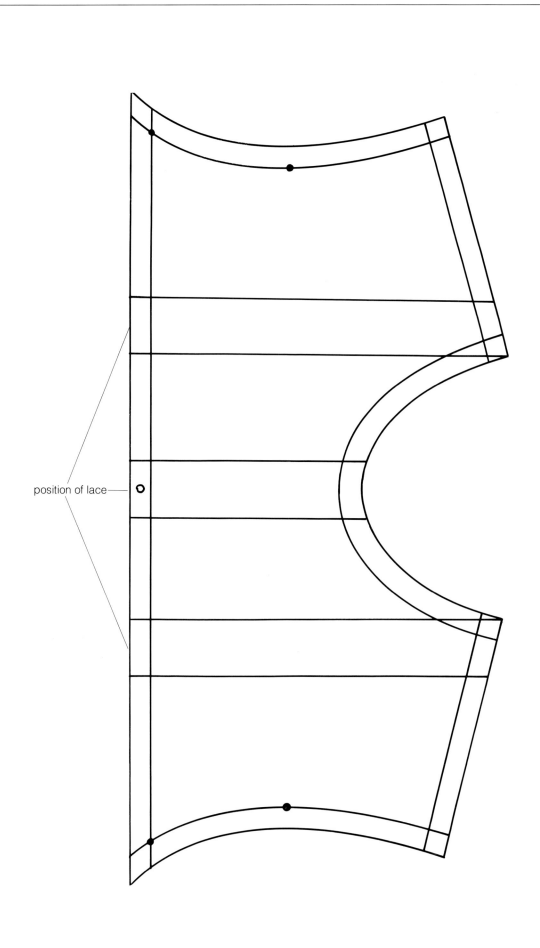

position of lace

Christening Robe (page 93): front yoke

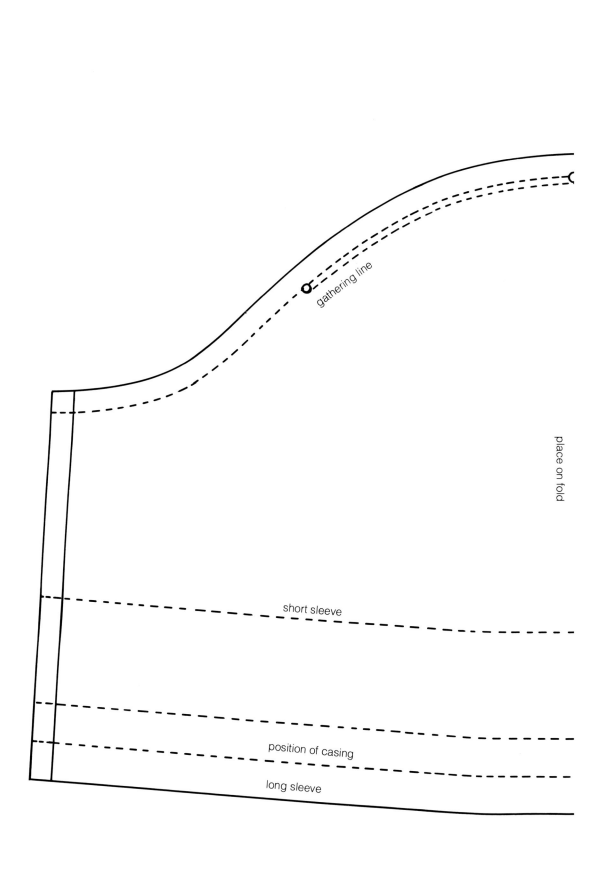

gathering line

place on fold

short sleeve

position of casing

long sleeve

Christening Robe (page 93): sleeve

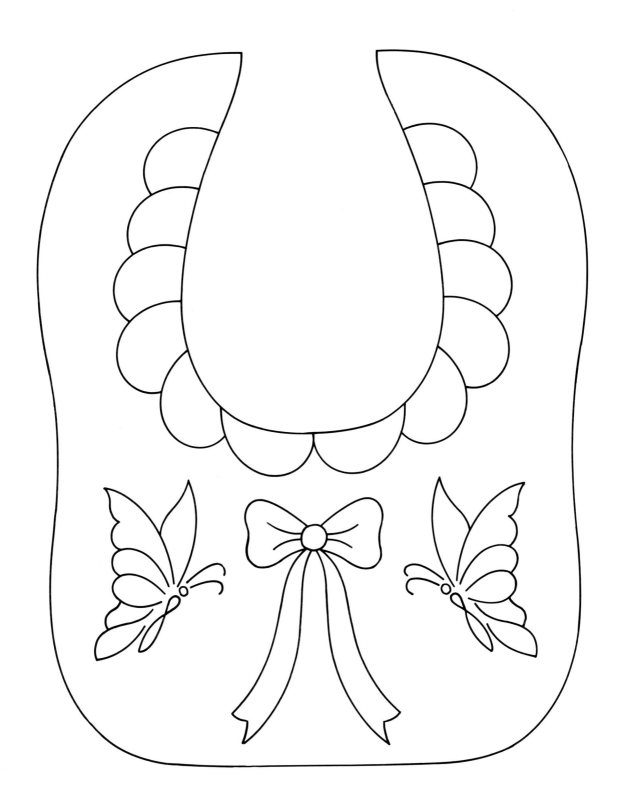

Christening Bib (page 96)

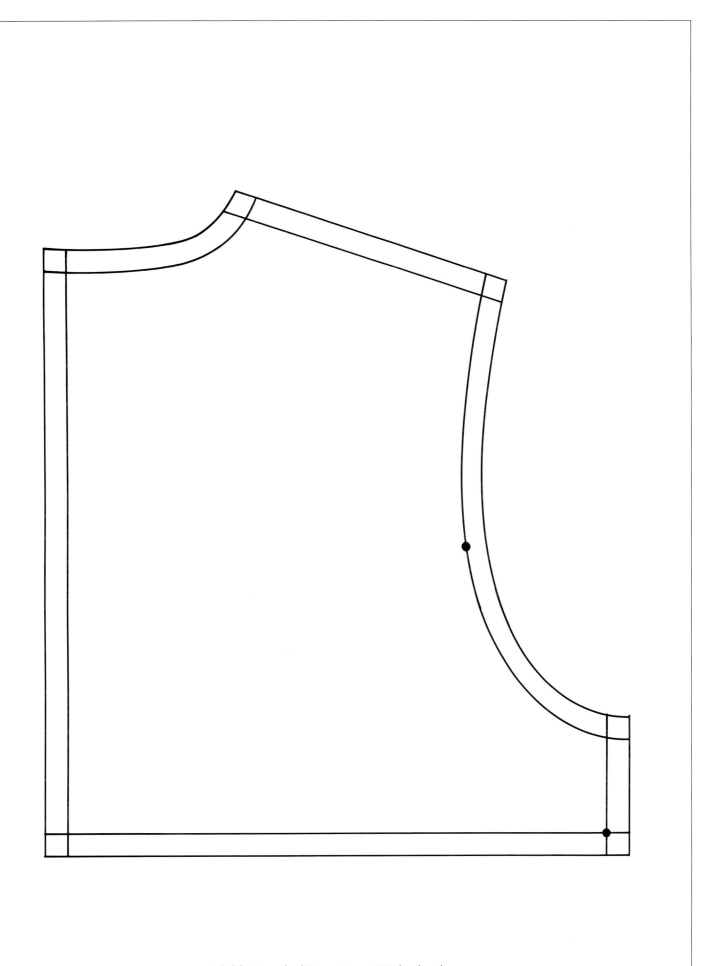

Child's Smocked Dress (page 96): back yoke

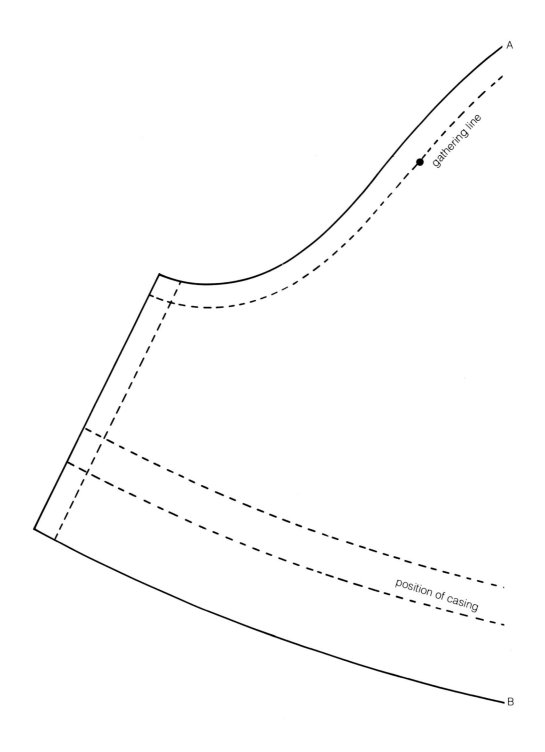

A

gathering line

position of casing

B

Child's Smocked Dress (page 96): sleeve (join to pattern on opposite page,
matching points A and points B, to obtain complete sleeve pattern)

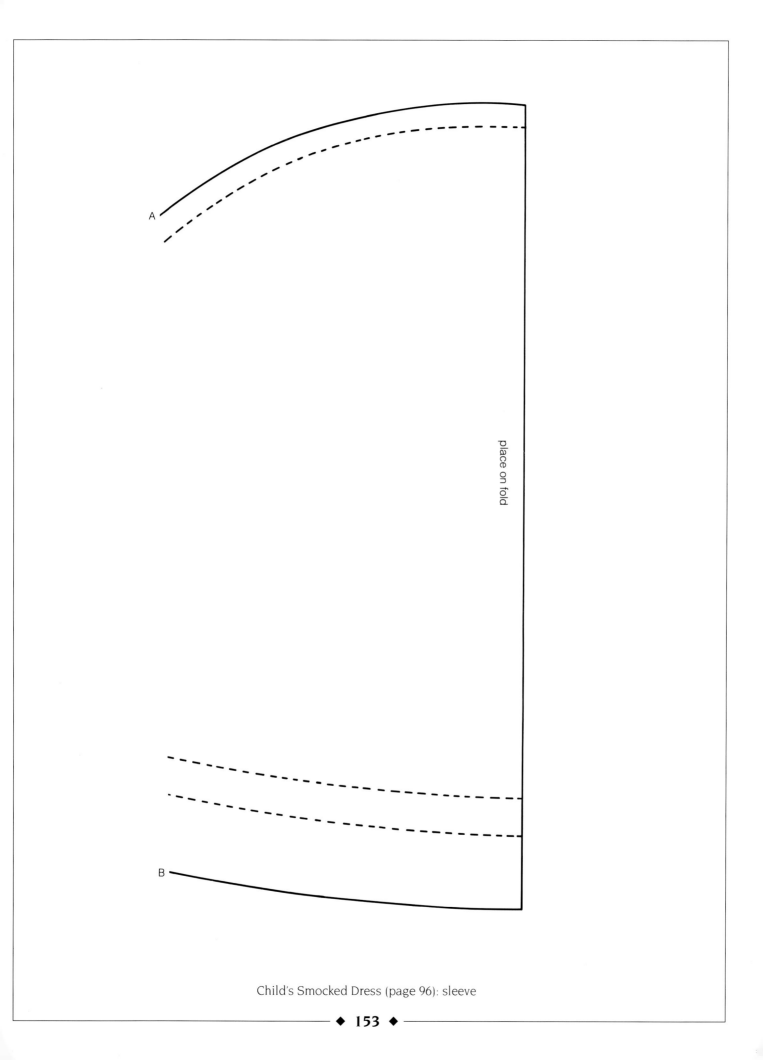

A

place on fold

B

Child's Smocked Dress (page 96): sleeve

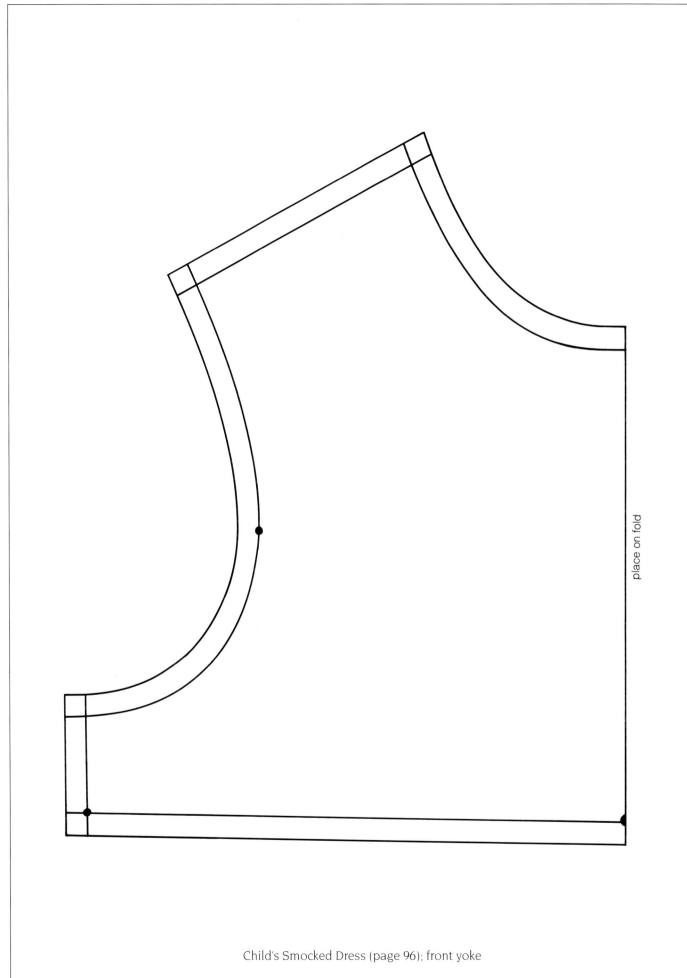

place on fold

Child's Smocked Dress (page 96); front yoke

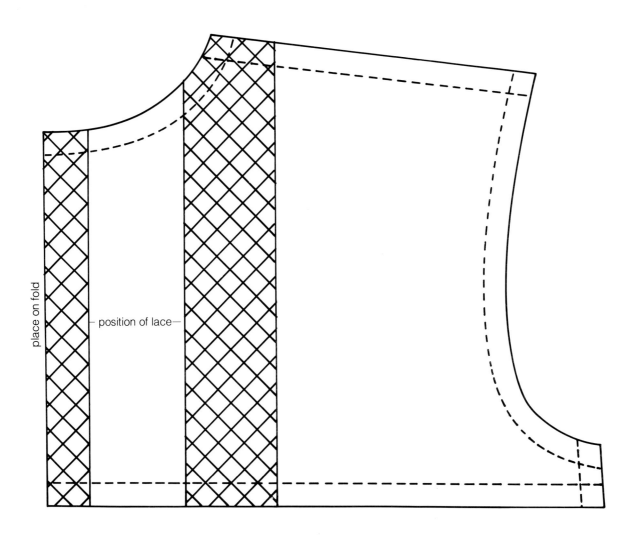

place on fold

position of lace

Child's Pinafore (page 98): bodice front

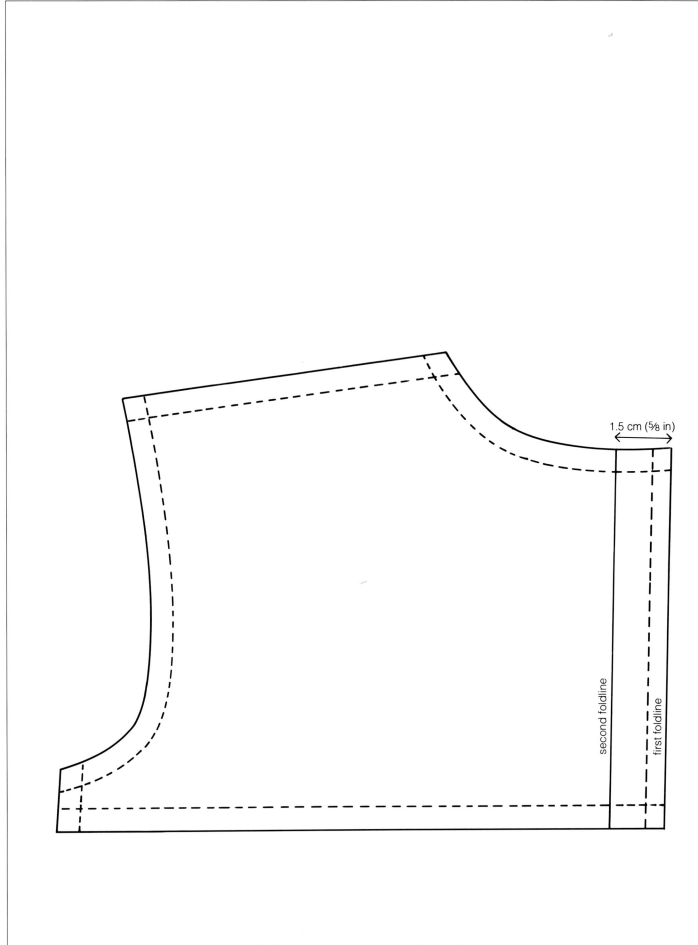

1.5 cm (⅝ in)

second foldline

first foldline

Child's Pinafore (page 98): bodice back

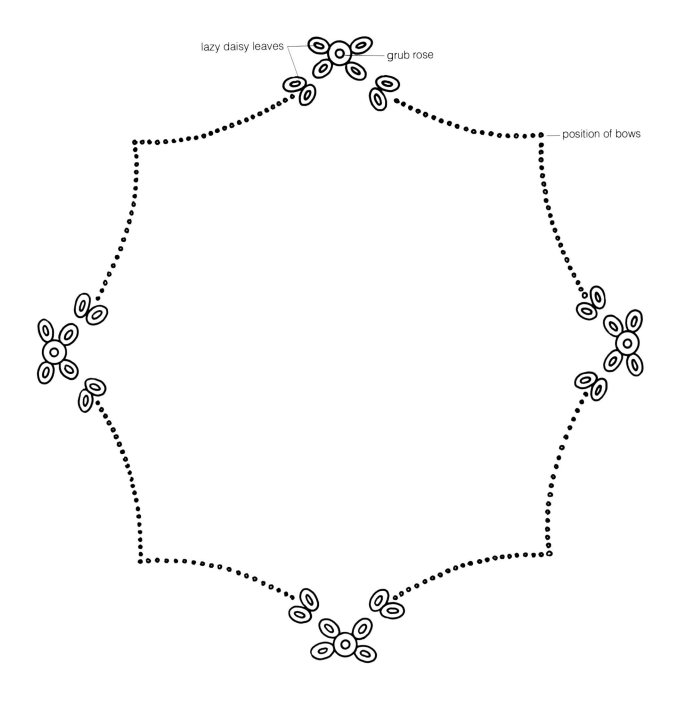

lazy daisy leaves

grub rose

position of bows

Lace Window Decoration (page 102)

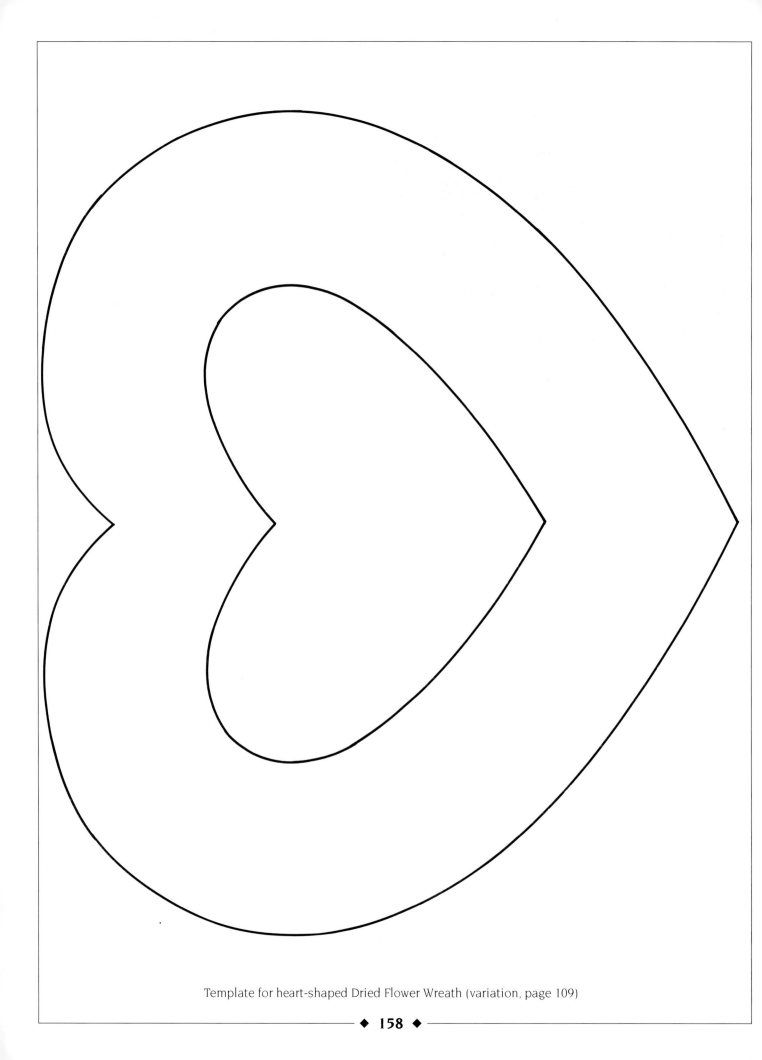

Template for heart-shaped Dried Flower Wreath (variation, page 109)

Template for Lace Coaster (page 104)

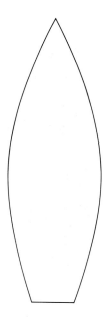

Template for Red Poinsettia (page 110)

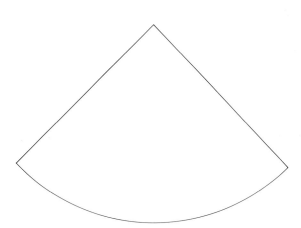

Template for Father Christmas's hat (page 110)

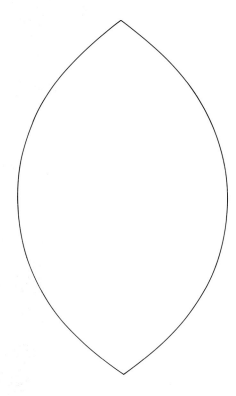

Template for Patchwork Ball (page 111)

Hoops for embroidery and quilting
and additional sets of designs are
available from:
Willowtree Products cc,
P O Box 103, Somerset West 7130.
Tel: (024) 85•24914

·INDEX·

Entries in *italics* refer to sewing projects.

A

antimacassar 83
  variation 83

B

back stitch 20, 34
bathroom, projects for 73–75
batting *see* wadding
bed cover, quilted 50–51
bedroom, projects for 45–71
bib, christening 96
binding, continuous, making 51
blanket stitch 15
blind, ruched 74–75
bow, double or multiple, making 101
bullion stitch 15
bullion stitch roses 26
button loops, making 43
buttonhole stitch 15

C

cable stitch 15
  single and double 28
calico 8
candlewick embroidery 19–21
  fabric 20
  hoop 20
  needles 20
  stitches 20–21
  thread 20
  quilting of 21
candlewicked, cushion cover 66
  mirror surround 68–69
  quilts 54–62
    with sashing 56–59
    without sashing 60–62
chain stitch 20
  twisted 17
chevron stitch 26
child's, pinafore 98–99
  smocked dress 96–98
christening, bib 96
  petticoat 95
  robe 93–94
Christmas cracker, lacy handkerchief 104
Christmas decorations *see* decorations and gifts
cinnamon decoration 108
clothing for babies and children 93–99
coasters, lace 104
colonial knot 21
cone wreath 108
continuous binding, making 51
coral stitch 15
corded or Italian quilting 32–35
coverlet, quilted crib 85
crib, *cover* 89
  doll's, pillowslip 91
  quilt 90
  or pram pillowslip 86
  sheet 87
  skirt and petticoat 88–89
cushion, cover, attaching front to back 43
  with pintucks, ribbon and lace 63
  lace 64–65
  lacy handkerchief 63
  quilted 81
  smocked 80
  inside, making 43

D

decorations and gifts 101–112
designs
  enlarging or reducing 11
  inspiration for 10
  planning and positioning for smocking 26
  tracing on to fabric 10
detached chain stitch *see* lazy daisy stitch
diamond stitch *see* chevron stitch
doily cone 105
doll's crib, pillowslip 91
  quilt 90
double fabric ruffle for round mirror 70
dress, child's smocked 96–98
dried flower(s), and pot-pourri 106
  wreath 109

E

embroidery 13–19
  beginning and ending off 14
  needles 14
  scissors 14
  stitches 15–17
  thread 14
  washing and ironing 14
English quilting 32–35
enlarging a design 11
equipment, and materials for needlework 8–11

F

fabric 8
  backing, for quilting 32
  for candlewicking 20
fabric door garland 101–102
Father Christmas, pine-cone 110
feather stitch 15
  for smocking 27
fishbone stitch 16
French knot 21
French seam 43
frill, making and attaching 42

G

garland, door 101–102

H

hand towel 73
hoops, embroidery and quilting 8, 20, 32

I

Italian or corded quilting 32–35

L

lace, working with 37–39
  coasters 104
  curtains 39
  cushion cover 64–65
  fan 105
  fan tree decoration 103
  gathering 39
  heart 103
  insertion 38
  mitring 39
  preparing for sewing 38
  storing 38
  window decoration 102
lace-edged net crib cover 89

lacy handkerchief Christmas cracker 104
lacy handkerchief cushion cover 63
lampshade, lacy tiffany 71
lazy daisy stitch 16
left-handers, instructions for 8
living-room, projects for 78–83
long and short stitch 16

M

mitring, corners of fabric 43
  lace 39
muslin 32

N

narrow hemming foot 9
needles 8, 20, 24, 32
nightdress case 66
  variation 67–68
nursery, projects for 85–91

O

outline stitch 16
  for smocking 28

P

patchwork ball 111
Pekinese stitch 16
petticoat, and skirt for crib 88–89
  christening 95
pillowslip, calculating fabric requirements 46
  crib or pram 86
  doll's crib 91
  frill, calculating fabric requirements 46
  to match sheet 47–48
  with lace insertions and embroidery 48
  with wide insertion 49
pinafore, child's 98–99
pincushion 112
pine-cone Father Christmas 110
pins 8
placket, making 42
pleater, smocking 24
polyester stuffing 32, 43
pot-pourri, and dried flowers 106
  sachets 107

Q

quilt(s), *bed cover* 50–51
  candlewicked, measurement charts for 52–53
    with sashing 56–59
    without sashing 60–62
  determining overall dimensions 54
  crib coverlet 85
  doll's crib 90
quilted cushion cover 81
quilting 31–35
  backing fabric for 32
  English 32–35
  hoop 32
  Italian or corded 32–35
  of candlewicked projects 21
  needles for 32
  preparing for 32
  stitches 33–34
  thimble 32
  thread 32
  Trapunto or stuffed 32–35
  yarn 32

R

red poinsettia 110
reducing a design 11
Roumanian stitch 17
ruched blind 74–75
ruffler foot 9
running stitch 17, 34
  threaded 17

S

sachet(s), pot-pourri 107
  Victorian handkerchief 107
satin stitch 21
scissors 8, 14
scroll stitch 17
sheaf stitch 17
sheet, calculating fabric requirements 45
  crib 87
  with insertions, pintucks and embroidery 45–46
smocked, dress, child's 96–98
  lampshade 81
smocking 23–29
  dot transfers 24, 25
  fabric for 24
  needles for 20
  pleater 24, 25
  setting pleats 29
stem stitch 21
  for smocking 28
stitches
  candlewicking 20–21
  embroidery 15–17
  quilting 33–34
  smocking 26–29
stuffed quilting or Trapunto 32–35

T

tablecloth, fitted round 77–78
  round ruffled 79
thimble 8, 32
thread 10, 20, 24, 32
threaded running stitch 17
towel, bath 73
  hand 73
tracing medium 10
transfers, smocking dot 24
Trapunto or stuffed quilting 32–35
trellis stitch *see* wave stitch
twisted chain stitch 17

V

Van Dyke stitch 29
Victorian handkerchief sachet 107

W

wadding 8, 32
wave stitch 29
wreath, cone 108
  dried flower 109
  variation 109
  willow or vine 108

Y

yarn 32

Z

zip, inserting in back of cushion cover 42